Where God, soul, and brother
are united in the right way,
there is the Kingdom of God.

A Ragaz Reader

SIGNS
OF THE
KINGDOM

Edited and Translated by

PAUL BOCK

With a Foreword by M. Douglas Meeks

William B. Eerdmans Publishing Company
Grand Rapids, Michigan

To Ben, Tim, and Jane

Library of Congress Cataloging in Publication Data:

Ragaz, Leonhard, 1868–1945.
  Signs of the kingdom.

  Translated from the German.
  Bibliography: p. 127
    1. Kingdom of God—Addresses, essays, lectures.
  2. Theology—Addresses, essays, lectures. 3. Socialism,
  Christian—Addresses, essays, lectures. I. Bock, Paul,
  1922–   . II. Title.
  BT94.R24213   1984   230′.42   84-8121
  ISBN 0-8028-1986-9

Contents

Foreword   vii
Acknowledgments   x
Introduction   xi

**PART I THE KINGDOM IN SOCIAL MOVEMENTS:
1887–1914**

The Gospel and the Current Social Struggle   3
Trip to America   16
Thy Kingdom Come   18

PART II THE KINGDOM AND VIOLENCE: 1914–1932

Not Religion but the Kingdom of God   27
The Kingdom of God and Clericalism   39
The Battle Against Bolshevism   43
Letter to President Wilson   47
Socialism and Violence   49
The Christian Revolution   64
Wilson and Lenin   66
A Remnant Will Remain   68
Which World View Belongs to Socialism?   75

PART III THE KINGDOM IN THE BIBLE: 1933–1945

Reformation Forward or Backward?   99
The Apostles' Creed   102
Israel, Judaism, and Christianity   105
The Ten Commandments   108
The Lord's Prayer   112
The Waiting   114
The Bible: An Interpretation   118

Selected Bibliography   127

Foreword

THIS FIRST EXTENSIVE TRANSLATION of works by Leonhard Ragaz will be welcomed in English-speaking countries. There will be widespread scholarly interest in these writings because of Ragaz's influence on and conflict with Karl Barth and other leading theologians and church leaders of this century. Many North American and British readers know the name Ragaz and its association with the Blumhardts. But whereas large portions of the Blumhardt texts have been available in English (see, for example, *Thy Kingdom Come: A Blumhardt Reader,* edited by Vernard Eller), Paul Bock has performed a much-needed service in selecting and so ably translating this collection of Ragaz texts.

A major interest in this book will be its focus on Ragaz's elaboration of his peculiar brand of religious socialism. The selection provides a chronological tracing of his developing thought. Ragaz regularly wrote in such a lucid and self-revealing way that one has here ready access to the personal, spiritual, and intellectual struggles in which he was involved until the end of his life. Thus it will now be possible to discern more precisely the differences between Ragaz's religious socialism and that of Paul Tillich, for example. Even though Ragaz's early criticism of religion sounds very similar to Barth's, these texts show how decisively the two departed in terms of their basic theology. The comparison of Ragaz and Barth will also throw light on Barth's lifelong identity as a socialist.

This book, however, will not only attract a scholarly interest for its considerable contribution to the study of twentieth-century theology. It also has a fresh, contemporary appeal. Despite the fact that they belong to the Swiss environment of the first four decades of this century, these texts often read as if they had been written in the midst of the current intensifying debates on faith and economics, war and peace, and so on. The issues dealt with here are still the pressing ones: poverty, exploitation, unemployment, greed, profligacy, violence, and corruption in the international political and economic order.

Readers may see in these essays adumbrations of current political and liberation theologies with their emphasis on praxis. And indeed, while he does not achieve their methodological sophistication, Ragaz does nevertheless describe for the life of ordinary people what the contemporary praxis theologies call for. For Ragaz theology was not a matter of delivering doctrinal deposits from the past or working out speculative principles.

Rather, he conceived of theology as a means to serve the conversion of people to God's righteousness as they engaged in the praxis of justice for the poor and oppressed.

Especially after he gave up his professorship, Ragaz began to address his theology specifically to the concerns of those who most suffered from exploitative economic structures. The passion of his work came from his suffering with their sufferings. His contact with those for whom participation in the economic system had led to the destruction of family life, crushed dreams, alcoholism, criminality, and the indignity of alienation from the community was the counterpoint of his absorption in the question of God's justice. For Ragaz the rule of God's righteousness always begins with the "least of these." That meant that all politics and economics — including the labor movement and all forms of socialism — had to be judged by whether those most subject to oppression and death were being given life by the movement or institution in question. The same criterion, Ragaz argued tirelessly, had to be applied to the church as well.

Ragaz was rancorously criticized throughout his career by the popular press for his socialist and antimilitarist stands. But for the most part these criticisms read into Ragaz's writings precisely what he was not saying. Ragaz was a severe critic of Bolshevism and materialistic Marxism, and he so often upheld the freedom and dignity of individual persons that some readers will be introduced here to an understanding of "socialism" that seems the intensification and integration of many strands of the Christian tradition. Few in the modern world have so realistically and concretely interpreted the gospel's understanding of work, property, and consumption and its implications for the modern industrial society. Only when seen in this light will Ragaz's boldness in pointing to God's rule in certain socialist movements be fully appreciated.

Ragaz will not be understood at all if he is not understood as preeminently a *theo*logical thinker. His one all-absorbing theme is All Glory to God! Behind everything he says is the call to holiness before the holy God. He does not criticize existing institutions and conditions according to the best principles of social theory but according to the will of God.

Ragaz's criticism of militarism, for example, was not built upon abstract principles of pacifism but on an intuitive knowledge of the demonic character of all human power. He did not condemn force itself, but made a distinction between force that exists merely to serve the ends of the state or certain interests of society and force that serves the establishment of freedom and justice on the basis of law. The spirit of militarism was a religious issue, for in it Ragaz saw the human urge to absolute power. The modern state's militaristic striving is from the perspective of the gospel a form of idolatry, a denial of the living God. Ragaz's vivid visions of what was coming as a result of this totalizing trust in military force were horrendously realized in the Second World War. Even before the nuclear age Ragaz could see that the tendency to worship security through military might could very well lead to the total destruction of the human project and of God's creation. Ragaz's careful analysis of militarism as sin is an important nonpacifist theological contribution in our time, when the logic of destroying the world in order to save the nation has become a commonplace of nuclear "realism."

In the manner of the Zwinglian tradition, Ragaz constantly reminded his fellow Swiss citizens that they owed their existence to a political form of the covenant that is grounded in justice. As a small nation, Switzerland should extend its spirit of solidarity to all other "small" nations and peoples who were subject to tyranny and dictatorship. The peculiar witness of the Swiss, according to Ragaz, would be their demonstration that a nation cannot live in fear if it expects to stay free from tyranny but rather must find its security in doing God's justice. So would Ragaz also teach us today.

M. Douglas Meeks

Acknowledgments

I WISH TO EXPRESS my thanks to the following:

To my wife Eve, a professor of German, who spent innumerable hours helping me with the translation.

To three American professors who gave me encouragement and advice as I worked on this reader: Dr. M. Douglas Meeks, Eden Theological Seminary, Webster Groves, Missouri; Dr. H. M. Rumscheidt, Atlantic School of Theology, Halifax, Canada; and Dr. Donald Dayton, Northern Baptist Theological Seminary, Lombard, Illinois.

To two Swiss professors who helped me select the material for translation: Dr. Markus Mattmüller, historian at the University of Basel and Ragaz's chief biographer; and Dr. Arthur Rich, social ethicist at the University of Zürich and Ragaz's chief theological and ethical interpreter.

To Dr. Christine Ragaz, daughter of Leonhard Ragaz, who provided me with many of her father's writings and who gave me helpful advice.

To Mrs. Virginia Penrose-Hirsekorn, secretary of the Junior Year at Heidelberg, Germany, for typing the manuscript.

To the Aigler Foundation at Heidelberg College, Tiffin, Ohio, for a travel grant.

To the Ragaz family, which has the publishing rights for most of the Ragaz publications, for permission to use the Ragaz documents.

To the Rotapfel-Verlag, Zürich, for permission to translate and publish portions from their publications *Dein Reich komme* and *Weltreich, Religion und Gottesherrschaft,* appearing in the selections "Thy Kingdom Come," "Not Religion but the Kingdom of God," and "The Kingdom of God and Clericalism."

To the Verlag Peter Lang, Bern, for permission to translate and publish portions from their publications *Das Reich und die Nachfolge* and *Gleichnisse Jesu,* appearing in the selections "A Remnant Will Remain" and "The Waiting."

Paul Bock
Doane College
Crete, Nebraska

Introduction

LEONHARD RAGAZ was born on July 28, 1868, the fifth of nine children of Bartholome and Luzia Ragaz, a farming couple in Tamins, a small mountain village in Canton Graubuenden in the German-speaking part of Switzerland. Through work on his parents' farm and hikes in nearby mountains and valleys, he developed a deep love for nature. He absorbed the democratic atmosphere of a Swiss village and remained for life a staunch believer in democracy. He was also impressed by the cooperative forms of economic life practiced by Swiss mountain farmers, and this experience later helped to shape his convictions about a decentralized form of socialism.

His father held a number of offices in the community and manifested a great interest in current affairs; this interest in politics was passed on to Leonhard. The family was constantly in financial difficulties; and so the children learned about social problems from personal experience.

After completing the basic schooling in Tamins, young Ragaz went to the cantonal high school in nearby Chur. He received little religious instruction at home, nor did the religion classes at school have much effect on him. His decision to study theology was a pragmatic one: there were scholarships available for it. He enrolled at the University of Basel, spent some time at the universities in Jena and in Berlin, and then returned to Basel. While in Germany, he became a great admirer of German culture, especially of German literature and art, but also a severe critic of Prussian militarism, which he had a chance to observe in Berlin.

The theological stance that he developed in his university years was that of liberalism, especially Hegelianism. It was above all the Swiss Hegelian theologian A. E. Biedermann who exerted a great influence on him. Somewhat pantheistic in his views, young Ragaz saw God in all nature and history.

In 1890 he was ordained as a Reformed pastor and began his ministry in three villages on the slopes of the mountain Heinzenberg in Canton Graubuenden, preaching, as he said himself, an "undogmatic Christianity." He began a very extensive study of the Bible — an activity he continued throughout his life — and labored to realize the "priesthood of all believers" by involving the laity more fully in the life of the church. Though very active in community affairs, he continued to read extensively and kept exploring more fully the writings of Hegel and other philosophers.

He also discovered that Kierkegaard's critique of the institutional church matched to a great degree with his own views.

Partly for health reasons and partly because of dissatisfaction, Ragaz temporarily gave up the ministry and between 1893 and 1895 served as a language and religion teacher in Chur. His readings in this period included books on Christian socialism, especially those written by English authors including Carlyle, Kingsley, and Robertson, and by German authors, especially Naumann. At this time he also became involved in the temperance movement and continued to be active in it for the rest of his life.

In 1895 he returned to the pastorate, accepting the position of senior pastor in Chur. He served there from 1895 to 1902. The influence of Kierkegaard and other writers led him to become more critical of liberalism, which was often interpreted as nothing more than "free thought." He manifested a great interest in ethics and gave several lectures to ministers' gatherings. In this period he was influenced by his reading of Albrecht Ritschl. While in Chur he married Clara Nadig, who proved to be a supportive companion in the many conflicts of his life.

In his ministry in Chur he came into direct contact with poverty, and he became aware of the interrelationships among bad housing, miserable working conditions, broken families, criminality, and alcoholism. There he discovered the social and structural dimensions of evil. Later he wrote about the "comprehensive solidarity of guilt." Becoming involved in educational programs for workers, he helped to found a center for workers with an alcohol-free restaurant and hotel, conference rooms, and a library. After giving a talk to a workers' group, he was given Karl Marx's *Das Kapital* as an expression of appreciation. In the final years in Chur Ragaz was very much in demand for public addresses, and he also received calls from several churches, but he turned them all down until in 1902 he received a call from the Münster (Cathedral) in Basel, which he decided to accept. He hoped that in that position he would have more time for reading and scholarly work than he had had in Chur.

Near the end of the stay in Chur and at the beginning of the ministry in Basel, Ragaz experienced an acute spiritual crisis. Political events at that time conflicted with his theology of history. Convinced that justice was on the side of the Boers in the Boer War, he could not accept the English victory. Why did God, the ruler of history, allow this? Through agonizing over this question he came to a deeper understanding of the cross and its application to history. He realized that justice does not always win in the short run. Disasters and setbacks can be used by God for the spiritual development of his people. Ultimately victory will come; that is the hope of Easter. There are many Good Fridays and many Easters in history. Ragaz's thinking moved from idealistic philosophy to Christology.

Study and experience in Basel led him to discover that the Kingdom of God for this earth was the central teaching of Christianity. He also came to see that the process of its development is not linear. There are catastrophes along the way. He saw, too, that the Kingdom is a gift of God, yet man participates in the coming, in the events that point to the ultimate coming: "Where God, soul, and brother are united in the right way, there is the Kingdom of God." It can be seen in secular as well as religious movements. Where people work for justice, freedom, and brotherhood, there are the signs of the Kingdom. One of the most hopeful signs for Ragaz was the labor movement.

Having begun his contacts with the labor movement in Chur, Ragaz continued them in Basel. In 1903 there was a great bricklayers' strike. Troops were called in. On the Sunday after Easter of that year Ragaz preached a sermon that came to be known as the "Bricklayers' Strike Sermon." He claimed that Christ was on the side of the oppressed, that the social movement had to do with the "humanization of humans" and thereby was a sign of the Kingdom of God, and that Christians should join in the struggle for the oppressed. The sermon was printed, widely distributed, and evoked both positive and negative reactions.

In that same year, when he took part in an Evangelical Social Congress in Darmstadt, Ragaz had an opportunity to establish contact with Germans engaged in the social struggle. He was particularly impressed by Wilhelm Herman's address.

Through the "Bricklayers' Strike Sermon" Ragaz became known as a friend of socialists. Shortly thereafter he came into contact with the Zürich pastor Hermann Kutter, and together they founded a new religious-social movement to help bring about the humanization of humanity. Three years earlier Kutter had issued the book *Sie müssen,* which made a strong impact on Switzerland. In it he charged that the social movement was doing more to realize God's purposes in history than the church, and he called upon the church to recognize God's work in the social movement. In 1906 Ragaz made an important address to a gathering of Swiss pastors, "Das Evangelium und der soziale Kampf der Gegenwart," in which he analyzed the social struggle and challenged Christians to become involved in it.

In 1907 Ragaz accepted an invitation to give an address to the World Congress of Free Christianity, which was meeting in

Boston. While in America he learned about Walter Rauschen-busch and the social gospel and later established contact with him. Mrs. Ragaz translated Rauschenbusch's *Christianity and Social Crisis* into German.

In 1908 Ragaz accepted a call to become Professor of Systematic and Practical Theology at the University of Zürich. While there he played a prominent role in the theological faculty and exercised an influence that went far beyond the city. Emil Brunner, who as a founder of dialectical theology took a direction different from that of Ragaz, later looked back on his student years and wrote, "That was a great time, when Ragaz came to Zürich. Then theology was interesting, not as a science, but as a proclamation in our time, as encounter with historical reality, with the labor question, with the war issue."

Ragaz maintained many international contacts with like-minded people in England, America, France, Germany, and elsewhere. In 1909 he had his first direct contact with Christoph Blumhardt of Bad Boll in Germany, and, like Kutter and Barth, he was greatly influenced by him. Blumhardt's eschatological "waiting for the Kingdom" also had an activist and social dimension. Blumhardt saw in the labor movement and in socialism signs of the coming Kingdom, and for a time he was deeply engaged in the social struggle. Ragaz's Christology was deepened through his contact with the man.

The many people influenced by Blumhardt each tended to emphasize a different part of his message. Kutter saw the Kingdom solely as a movement from God to man. Ragaz distinguished between an "absolute hope" and a "relative hope" in the Kingdom. The absolute hope was based on God's action only; the relative hope—signs pointing to the Kingdom, such as movements for social justice—called for man's participation with God, and thus entailed movement originating from man as well as from God. The absolute hope, Ragaz believed, provided the standard for measuring the relative hope. Kutter took no part in secular movements, restricting himself to work within the church. He believed that the church had to be renewed before it could enter into the social struggle. Ragaz, on the other hand, was active in the labor movement and in politics. Their differences led to a conflict within the Swiss religious-socialist movement. Kutter accused Ragaz of politicizing the gospel; Ragaz felt that Kutter's theology led to quietism. Karl Barth later followed the path of Kutter more than that of Ragaz, though he respected Ragaz's activism.

In 1912 there was a general strike in Zürich, and again Ragaz became involved. He was particularly shocked by the attack of the military upon the workers, and this experience contributed to his later antimilitarist stand. His protest against the mistreatment of the workers evoked a corresponding protest against his activism: he was charged with proclaiming a "general strike theology." Efforts were made to remove him from his position at the University, but they were not successful.

In the same year Ragaz took part in an important event in Basel. The Peace Congress of the Socialist International met in the Münster. He spoke of how God was building his Kingdom with unchurched people who were doing what Christians ought to be doing. He became involved in the planning of a large world conference for social Christianity that was to be held in Basel in 1914. In preparation Ragaz made a trip to England in the spring of 1914, visited with a number of Christian socialists, and established contact with several settlement houses. The World War, however, prevented the conference from taking place.

The coming of the war was a great setback for the religious-socialist movement. The belief that international socialism could prevent a war proved to be an illusion. Workers in each country rallied to fight for their nation. Ragaz saw in the war God's judgment upon the world and upon Christianity and called for repentance and renewed dedication.

Swiss religious socialists were shocked by the way some German theologians were justifying the war, blending Christianity and nationalism. Both Ragaz and Barth had some sharp written exchanges with certain German theologians. For Ragaz the problem of violence increasingly became the matter of major concern. Before 1914 it was socialism; afterwards it was violence. He believed that Christians must battle against everything that rests on violence because violence belongs to the kingdom of evil. Earlier, while studying in Germany, he had developed an antipathy for militarism as he saw it there. Unlike Kutter, who hoped for a German victory, Ragaz hoped for a German defeat. But he also gave much attention to the events in Switzerland, noting the profound influence upon it by the large neighboring powers. In his most popular book, *Die neue Schweiz,* he called upon the Swiss to be true to their democratic heritage and to make a distinctive contribution to the world. Even so, Ragaz saw nationalism as one cause of militarism.

In his struggle to work for peace and against the intoxicating power of militarism, Ragaz sought to begin with men's souls. He fostered various peace plans, among which was the establishment of a Peace Sunday in Swiss churches. His wife, Clara, was involved in peace movements before her marriage and continued her activity thereafter. She was one of the Swiss representatives at a conference of peace groups from neutral nations held in Sweden in 1916.

Ragaz distinguished between two types of pacifism and saw a place for both. There was the absolute pacifism of Tolstoi, manifested in the witness of conscientious objectors, whom he strongly supported as witnesses for the Kingdom of God and against violence. And there was a relative pacifism, the sort expressed in political and diplomatic internationalism. Despite his support for conscientious objectors, Ragaz was himself more a relative pacifist, working hard for an international organization. An admirer of Woodrow Wilson, he supported Wilson's League of Nations plan wholeheartedly. He did not think that conscientious objection was a feasible policy for the majority of any nation's population to follow. He hoped that someday it might be possible for a whole nation to lay down its weapons, but he doubted that it was a feasible option for the present. There are occasions, he said, when individuals and nations must defend themselves.

As was noted earlier, Ragaz saw the World War as a judgment upon the world and upon Christianity. It was in this time of crisis that his attacks on the institutional church became sharper than ever. Like Barth after him, he developed a very negative concept of the word *religion,* though he gave it a different meaning than Barth did. For Ragaz, religion came to mean the church consecrating a corrupt social order, playing with people's sentiments, focusing on the next world, developing static dogmas and rigid institutions. He set the Kingdom of God over against religion, the prophetic over against the priestly. As he saw it, people who were related to the Kingdom read the signs of the times and acted accordingly. Many of them were not in the church but in progressive secular movements. In his writings Ragaz strongly attacked the union of religion and power, which he called "Pfaffentum" (clericalism). He saw in the New Testament the development of a Christian community or Kingdom community but not of a church, and in history he found more signs of such Christian community in the sects and heresies than in the established churches.

After 1913 Ragaz was active in the Swiss Social Democratic Party and exerted a considerable influence in it. The hopes of the Socialist International having been destroyed by the war, Swiss socialists looked for new directions. Various options were debated in the Swiss Social Democratic Party during the war, among them Bolshevism. Trotsky came to Switzerland to express his views, and Ragaz had a stimulating encounter with him, although he expressed himself very strongly against Bolshevism, especially in his pamphlet "Sozialismus und Gewalt." He saw Bolshevism, with its reliance on violence, as a complete betrayal of socialism. The religious-social movement was instrumental in persuading Swiss socialists not to join the Communist International.

After 1916 the religious-social movement showed signs of decline. This was due partly to the conflict between Ragaz and Kutter and partly to Ragaz's rejection of dialectical theology.

In his *Römerbrief,* Barth rejected any kind of identification of the Kingdom of God with a secular movement. It was all right to be a Social Democrat, but it was not all right to be a religious-social advocate. In 1919 Ragaz was invited to give a lecture at a religious-social conference in Tambach, Germany. When he was unable to attend for health reasons, Barth was invited to take his place. He gave a major lecture in which he attacked any kind of "hyphenated Christianity," whether Christian-social, evangelical-social, or religious-social, on the grounds that they all lead to the secularization of Christianity. The church must proclaim a God who is "wholly other," who stands over against man and all movements, he said. God brings the Kingdom in his own way; people do not organize it.

Before long, a clear break took place between dialectical theology and religious socialism. The former was stressing the Word of God; the latter, the reality of God in the world. For Barth, God's work in the church was more important; for Ragaz, it was God's work in the world that was preeminent. Both drew insights from Blumhardt, but they went in different directions. Many theological students and pastors became followers of dialectical theology and abandoned the religious-social movement. This was a bitter experience for Ragaz. He felt that dialectical theology was reactionary, quietistic, antihumanistic; and he felt that his own theology was misunderstood. He had not identified the Kingdom of God with social movements; these were only signs of the coming Kingdom. Furthermore, he distinguished between relative and absolute hopes of the Kingdom. His critics, however, felt that in practice his relative hopes sounded too much like absolutes.

Ragaz continued to be influenced by Blumhardt's writings. In 1921 he published *Der Kampf um das Reich Gottes in Blumhardt, Vater und Sohn — und weiter!,* an anthology of writings of the two Blumhardts, father and son, with his own commentary. The book reveals how much Ragaz's thinking was in line with the thinking of the Blumhardts.

An important change took place in Ragaz's life in 1921. He had become increasingly disillusioned with the institutional church and did not believe that it could be an instrument of the Kingdom—at least not until it had experienced radical reform. He found more hope in secular movements such as the labor movement and in small groups of committed Christians who could read the signs of times. He felt that he had to act according to his beliefs, so he gave up his position on the theological faculty, moved from an upper-class into a predominantly working-class section of Zürich, and set up an educational center there. He planned to establish a settlement house there, too, but for financial reasons was unable to do so. The educational center did not reach large numbers. The program included evening Bible studies in which he interpreted current events in light of the Scriptures. He spent the rest of his life working at the center and editing the journal *Neue Wege.*

Through the *Neue Wege* Ragaz continued to present his call for social change in light of his belief in the Kingdom of God. A cause that he championed with particular ardor was that of the League of Nations. Along with several other Swiss leaders, he tried to persuade his country to join the League. He admired and corresponded with Woodrow Wilson, and sometimes pictured the world conflict as a choice between Wilson and Lenin. He wished that the world would take something from both— democracy from Wilson and socialism from Lenin. The University of Geneva awarded honorary doctorates to Wilson and Ragaz in the same year. Upon the death of Wilson, Ragaz was called upon to conduct the memorial service for him in Zürich.

Ragaz criticized the Versailles Peace Treaty, finding it too harsh, and saw in it the seeds of future conflict. He became a strong supporter of disarmament conferences and urged his country to take leadership in the disarmament cause. As the disarmament conferences failed and the League proved helpless against aggressors, Ragaz wrote less about disarmament and more about the undemocratic spirit of militarism. As he worked for peace he maintained contact with people of other nations, among them Arthur Henderson, a British Labour Party politician, and Thomas Masaryk, the president of Czechoslovakia, who was a regular reader of the *Neue Wege.*

Responding to invitations to speak, Ragaz traveled widely in the twenties and thirties. He became particularly well known in Czechoslovakia, Holland, and Scandinavia. One book of his that appeared in several languages, *Von Christus zu Marx —von Marx zu Christus,* brought into focus his extensive thinking in regard to Christianity, socialism, and communism.

From the beginning of the emergence of fascism, Ragaz was its ardent foe. He attacked Italian fascism and later German

Nazism. He opposed both forms of totalitarianism—fascist or communist. He saw the failure of the League to stop aggression in Abyssinia as a foreboding and a disturbing sign. In defining his own views on violence he was often torn. He was not an absolute pacifist. In his view, nonviolence as taught by Gandhi had its place but required extensive preparation of the people. He fought militarism, yet recognized that aggression could not be stopped without collective security. He was appalled by England's and France's betrayal of Czechoslovakia at Munich, and when the Germans invaded Czechoslovakia, he called upon the Czechs to resist.

Ragaz wrote so strongly against Nazism that in the opinion of the authorities he threatened the national interests of a neutral country. For a time during the war he was forbidden to print his journal, but he found a way to issue and distribute it clandestinely.

In the late thirties and early forties Ragaz did considerable writing in the realm of biblical interpretation. He expressed his understanding of the Kingdom of God in books about the parables and the Sermon on the Mount, and particularly in a seven-volume Bible commentary, which was published posthumously. Much of what he wrote had already been expressed in the Bible study evenings in the workers' education center.

In his last years he saw his and Barth's positions come closer together. He was glad to see Barth's increasing involvement in political issues and welcomed the change in his theology. While in the early years Barth was stressing the distance between God and man, later he came to stress the incarnation. And Barth also changed his views on Ragaz. Professor Markus Mattmüller, Ragaz's chief biographer, spoke with Barth shortly after the latter had read the first published volume of Ragaz's letters. "It has become clear to me that this man was a passionate theologian who wrestled with the Gospel," said Barth. The volume "showed him to me in a new light."

Near the end of World War II, as the United Nations idea was advocated and as the San Francisco conference took place, Ragaz's hopes for peace were renewed. The emergence of the U.N. was a rainbow over the horrible destruction of the war.

Shortly before his death the atomic bombs were dropped on Hiroshima and Nagasaki. Ragaz saw this "Satanic Wonder" as a shocking sign that mankind stood before the final decision — either to find a way toward collective security through an effective United Nations and disarmament or to face world catastrophe.

On December 6, 1945, Ragaz died, just after completing that month's issue and with it the thirty-ninth volume of the *Neue Wege*. The journal continued to be published by his followers and in 1981 celebrated its seventy-fifth anniversary. Another journal of the religious-socialist movement, *Der Aufbau,* continues to be published by Ragaz's followers.

The contributions of Ragaz have been assessed by various authors. In his book *Leonhard Ragaz,* Andreas Lindt of Switzerland makes the following points:

1. He helped to awaken Christianity to its social responsibility and contributed much to Christian thought on economics, politics, and international affairs. The Swiss movement he inspired paralleled similar social movements in other countries, and together they created a concern that led to the formation of the Life and Work Movement, one of the antecedents of the World Council of Churches. The Swiss movement was particularly strong before World War I and would have been better known if the International Conference for Social Christianity planned for 1914 had taken place. Ragaz distinguished himself by his deep involvement in the social movements. He was no armchair social ethicist; he put his beliefs into action.

2. He contributed to the Christian understanding of God's action in history. His was not a hidden God, but a God who could be glimpsed at times in movements that contributed to the humanization of humans. (In this he was much like a later Catholic theologian, Pierre Teilhard de Chardin.) His critics felt that he claimed too much insight into history and in doing so came close to identifying the Kingdom of God with certain movements. He acknowledged that there were struggles and setbacks in history, that there were crucifixions, but for him they pointed toward Easter. His eschatological view of history anticipated a later development known as the Theology of Hope. He saw Jesus as being "not behind us but before us."

3. He contributed ideas concerning the role of Christians in a secularized world. He saw an anonymous Christianity working in the world, functioning quite differently than official institutional religion. Thus he anticipated some later thought about secular Christianity and worldly Christianity. However, in retrospect it appears that he had too little appreciation for the institutional church and his own indebtedness to it and to the church's continuing contribution to the realization of the values he cherished.

Dr. Josef Hromadka, a noted Czech theologian, urged his students to read both Barth and Ragaz, "to salt their Barth with some Ragaz," as he put it. He had a high regard for both men and felt that they supplemented and corrected each other. In his autobiography Hromadka wrote that Barth's theology corrected that of Ragaz, for there was the danger that biblical and church life would become replaced by political and social enthusiasm. On the other hand, he also felt that Ragaz corrected Barth's theology, which was in danger of becoming a school of churchly, systematized theology. He claimed that he had learned from both. "Ragaz remained for us the light in which we could see the limits of every theological system and churchly institution. We had to salvage something from Ragaz's dynamics of history for the new battles and tasks of the church."

In Jürgen Moltmann's "theology of hope" one can find a convergence of Barthian theology with some of Ragaz's concepts. In his book *Konzept einer sozialethischen Theorie,* Martin Honecker, a German theologian, has noted the similarities in the specific teachings of Ragaz and Moltmann. Both emphasize eschatology, the coming of the Kingdom, he says, and both give it a strong this-worldly emphasis. Both stress the biblical concept of a God who works in history, rather than the static, other-worldly Greek concept of God. Both talk of a God "who goes before us." Both criticize the existing religious institutions in light of the concept of the Kingdom of God. Both oppose the privatization of religion and stress social responsibility. Both are critical of Luther's "Two Kingdom theory." Both base their Kingdom hopes on Christ, especially on the cross and resurrection. Both develop their concepts of justice for this earth through coming to grips with the challenge of Marxism.

But Honecker also notes significant differences between the two. For Moltmann, socialism and democracy are *not* manifestations of the coming of the Kingdom, he suggests. Social responsibilities are undertaken in response to the Kingdom hope. Moltmann does not place the Kingdom of God and the church over against each other as Ragaz does; he does not carry on a polemic against theology and the church; nor does he play Jesus and Paul against each other as Ragaz does. Honecker also suggests that Ragaz's attack on Luther's theory is more extreme than Moltmann's, and that Ragaz has a more negative view of the state than Moltmann does. He also sees an element of anarchism in Ragaz.

It becomes apparent that some contemporary European theologians have developed their theologies partly by accepting the ideas of religious socialism and partly by reacting against them. In any case, one can understand contemporary theology better by understanding this movement as it is represented by Leonhard Ragaz.

When reading Ragaz's writings one realizes their relevancy to current problems. His efforts to develop a human socialism bear great similarity to the eastern European yearning for a

"Socialism with a human face" and to the Latin American interest in Christian socialism. His grappling with the problems of violence in revolutions brings to mind the current debate about violent revolution in the Third World, particularly the debate aroused by the World Council of Churches' Program to Combat Racism. And his stand against militarism and nationalism certainly has a bearing on current peace movements.

It is apparent that Leonhard Ragaz was a twentieth-century pioneer in the field of Christian social action.

PART I

The Kingdom
in Social Movements
1887–1914

Delivered at a pastors' conference in Basel in 1906, this address is a very important early statement by Ragaz, expressing his Kingdom-of-God theology and its social implications. It is one of the foundational documents of the religious-social movement that was founded in the same year.

In the following selection, sections I–II and IV–VII have been abridged. In section III, which is given in full, we can see how Ragaz applies to the existing social conflict the Christian ethic, with its twofold emphasis on the value of the individual and on brotherhood.

THE GOSPEL AND THE CURRENT SOCIAL STRUGGLE

OUR PRESENT SITUATION is a critical one, and it is time for religion to influence society. Four hundred years ago a religious personality, Niklaus von der Fluh, reconciled two parts of our country and prevented a war. In his spirit we need once again to bring a Christian influence to bear.

I

One needs to understand what is happening. Thus the first task is to clarify what is going on in the economic conflicts of our time. These conflicts between owner and worker, skilled laborer and unskilled laborer, rural people and urban people, women and men, reflect the differences in goals and methods of three stages of economic development — precapitalist, capitalist, and socialist.

II

What does the gospel of Jesus have to do with the economic conflict? A pietistic interpretation of the Bible can lead to conservatism. But a study of the Synoptic Gospels can lead to a more radical approach. The Kingdom of God is the central concept of the good news. Jesus teaches the worth of each child

3

of God as well as the brotherhood of men under God. Jesus sees Mammon as the greatest enemy of man.

III

Now the two great powers in question (capitalism and socialism) stand so clearly before us that their relationship to each other becomes obvious. How does the gospel of Jesus relate to the current economic struggle?

Before I try to give an answer, I would like to assert forcefully once again that we find it impossible to make a pure economic evaluation. We are not considering what the economic advantages and disadvantages of the present system are, or how it would be technically possible to replace it with another system. We are asking first of all, simply, Does the capitalistic system embody the way of life of the gospel, the basic implications of which we have sought to expound? My answer is a very decisive: No. It contradicts it so much that it strikes one in the face. It must be replaced with something better if the demands of the gospel are to be realized among men.

Now that I have bluntly presented my main thesis, I'd like to try to guard it against some misunderstandings. Naturally, I do not deny that under the domination of capitalism one can see himself as a child of God just as one was able to do during the rule of the heathen Roman Empire. But didn't the Christians then hope that the Kingdom of God would replace the Roman Empire? Even in an environment of alcoholism and prostitution, oppressed by incurable illness and neglected or kicked about by men, one can preserve the awareness that one is a child of God — and honor to the person that can do it! But who would therefore deny that these things are abominations before God and that Christians must therefore fight against them?

Also, I do not wish to forget to say that my criticism of capitalism does not necessarily apply to individual capitalists, who did not, after all, invent the system. It would be very presumptuous of us if we as pastors (who hopefully have nothing to do with speculation in the market, with dividends, or with workers' wages) assumed that we were better disciples of Jesus than merchants and entrepreneurs (who, it goes without saying, personally can be of the finest and noblest nature and, in fact, quite often are).

And one more point. What worthwhile things capitalism has achieved and will continue to achieve until its death should not go unrecognized. We will leave aside the irresolvable question of whether it was historically necessary, or if it could have developed differently; nor will we explore the question of whether its origins were good or bad. It is certain that it has waded in blood and wickedness, that it has sanctified the downfall of whole nations and brought immeasurable misery even to a large share of the exploiting nations, and that the pillars of its temple are distress, horror, curses of despair, and wrongs that cry to heaven. Perhaps it will be said that it intended to do evil but God has turned it to good, that the mountains of innocent victims it has slaughtered cannot have died in vain. And indeed, capitalism has to be given credit for bringing to light the riches of the earth in previously unheard-of ways. Through it alone it has been possible to feed the population of the West, which has tripled and quadrupled in the course of the last hundred years. Capitalism has brought within reach the ideal first proclaimed by Jesus and later restated by K. F. Meyer in a well-known poem — "that all shall be filled." Together with modern science it has unlocked fabulous powers that permit us to hope for even greater things to come. It has increased man's power to an unlimited degree. In its own way it has mastered nature and has made the material world subject to the spirit. To a large degree it has conquered space and time. It has held before man the prospect of freedom from slavery and drudgery and from soul-destroying anxiety about food. By fulfilling the condition that Aristotle jokingly established for the elimination of slavery—namely, that the weaver's shuttles run by themselves— it has created a better style of living and has awakened people from all kinds of dreary slumber to unprecedented activity and exertion of strength. Only in the capitalistic era has mankind learned what can be achieved through work. There were rather confined and often pretty dreadful conditions in what we call "the good old days"; from the religious and moral point of view it is not bad that the ideal of idyllic small-town life is gone. The old forms had become hardened and stiffened.

Nevertheless, capitalism has also brought an incredible unrest into the world. By destroying a whole world overnight and creating a new one, it showed to mankind in a previously unknown fashion *ad oculos* that neither economic nor other conditions have the permanence of a God-given natural order that man had earlier dreamed of. It has taught us to hope. In an enormous crisis it exposed all the injustice and sloth of the earlier social orders and thus introduced a new epoch for man. It is a strong *Excelsior.* In its own way it is a prophecy of the Kingdom of God.

If we, however, in looking at the negative side of this development, demand a still better economic order, then we must first of all avoid two misunderstandings. I say, "better economic order," not "industrial management." We cannot think of turning back to the old forms of manual labor, even though Ruskin, who has much to say about social questions, and his followers have such romantic dreams. It is important to take the engineering techniques and industrial forms that have been developed so well by capitalism (e.g., mass production) and make them serve man in a different and better way. The tools must not be changed, but rather the spirit in which the tools are used must be changed.

What shall we call this new order? Is it the socialist order? I could call it that, and sometimes I do, since I am convinced that socialism in its basic goals provides the direction that will lead us out of capitalism to the next higher level in historical development. But I do not wish to give the impression that I identify the teachings of Christ with a particular social order such as, for example, the socialistic one. In theory we certainly need to recognize the possibility that after socialism has made its contribution to the betterment of mankind, a new and better order can arise to serve this end. Our task is simply to determine which *telos* an economic order must have if it is to harmonize with the life-style required by the gospel, to measure it by this yardstick, and to formulate in broad outline our postulates for changing it. The future developments may appear in this form or that and may take on different names.

The first requirement is that an economic order *serve* man and not rule over him, for the worth of a human being qua human being is, as we can see, one of the two poles of the gospel ethic. Using gospel language we could say that the economic order should express or acknowledge the concept that man is a child of God. Thereby capitalism stands condemned. Its economic *telos* is, as we have seen, purely mechanical and impersonal: it centers on the increase of capital. The person, who according to the gospel and also according to Kant should never be treated simply as a means but always as a being of intrinsic value, is used simply as a means to greater profit. He is viewed as a being of lesser value than the machine because he is cheaper. In industrialized nations one does not speak anymore about workers but rather about "hands." Man is debased in the very place that should be the creative center of his moral self: at his work place.

Everything creative has been transferred to the machine. The machine has swallowed up individual personality; mechanism has proved to be victorious. Under these circumstances it is impossible to demand from workers a deep love for and loyalty to their work. How can these proletarians, tossed here and there by the winds of industrial life—who, to put it bluntly, have to beg for work — how can they achieve a deep-rooted spiritual existence? The situation is clear: the gospel calls for an economic order that makes the machine the slave and the man the master, as God would have it; the gospel speaks against all dehumanizing economic orders and in favor of all economic orders that give man his right as God's child and as king.

The gospel not only has an individual component but also a social component that demands that the economic order serve man and that man serve his fellowmen. Here again capitalism stands condemned, for it atomizes society. It is, of course, impersonal, but it is also thoroughly selfish (in an objective sense). To be sure, it tries to cover up its crass egoism with the argument that one who seeks one's own good simultaneously works for the common good. But in reality one makes oneself comfortable in this way only at the cost of defying God, whose moral order this argument clearly flouts. In the spirit of the gospel, we are debtors to all our brothers. This pertains also to work. A true Christian cannot tolerate wage slavery; he cannot stand and watch God's gift of work debase his fellow humans, watch it become a curse, watch it cause their souls to wither. It will pain him, and he will have to search for a new form through which sonship and brotherhood can find expression also in work.

Unfortunately, in this area some of the pioneers have been people who, though they were actually disciples of Christ, refused to be called Christians—people such as Robert Owen in England and Professor Abbe in Jena. People usually pass over the utopian views of the former with a smile, forgetting that he was doing pioneering work and that he succeeded in proving to the whole world that a highly developed industrial system is compatible with a goal other than the increase of capital — namely, with the realization of the good of the workers and of the whole community. The worker does have something to say about his work and has certain clearly defined rights as a member of the working community, which in turn takes its place in the larger community.

There can be a future in which the industrial feudal aristocracy will change into a democratic republic. Similar beginnings are sprouting up everywhere. The cooperatives and trade unions point in the same direction. One concrete example makes clear what the goal of the economy must be in the light of the gospel: not the aggrandizement of money for its own sake, not purely egoistic self-preservation, but rather a concerted effort to overcome material need. Thus the economic order becomes a way of realizing brotherhood. It becomes the means by which to realize the fullness of the social imperative of the gospel. It is no longer the patriarchal form of service whereby one only commands and the other only obeys, the relationship of master and slave, but rather a mutual service—a service, above all, of the strong to the weak, in humility and unselfishness. That is what it means to serve Jesus. It is to this level of service that patriarchal Christian groups should raise themselves. It is a higher ideal than the one they have been serving up to now and, to be sure, a more uncomfortable one. Nobody understands the times and the will of God who does not comprehend this.

The domineering point of view that we hear expressed from time to time — "I will be the master in my house (i.e., in my business)" — is false in every respect. What does the manufacturer want to do in his house if the house is empty? What can he do without workers? Doesn't the work have as much value as the capital? The old master could talk like this when he took responsibility for his servant and cared for him in sickness and in old age, but does the present-day employer have the right to talk that way when he often does not even know the worker? The complaints of housewives about their maids' diminishing interest in "service" likewise fail to recognize the change in their relationship. A new relationship must evolve among people, one based on equality and on the respect for one's own personality as well as the personality of the other person. This does not mean some sort of standardized equality. There will always be leaders and followers. The "equality" anticipated in some models of monolithic future states is not a worthwhile or necessary goal. But patriarchalism is gone; brotherhood is coming. Thus, even Carlyle's ideals are somewhat anachronistic. Serving must remain, but it has to be more highly valued and has to develop properly.

The whole of intellectual development is moving in this direction. Precisely the most important sociological, psychological, and ethical findings, which have been revealed to our generation more clearly than to any other, are urgently saying to us that we belong together. We know better than earlier generations how economic, moral, and religious conditions relate to one another. When we dig to expose the roots of the evil that oppresses us we always hit upon the collective guilt that each one of us must bear a part of. If we look for help, we recognize that we will find it only through working together. The great needs that social criticism has identified in recent decades call for far-reaching and cohesive responses. Out of the depth of knowledge and experience of our times comes the call for alliance in the battle for a better humanity.

The economic order also has to fit into this new picture of human nature. In the preindustrial society each person supported himself through independent work; in the capitalistic era people were brought together for a common work. There developed powerful associations, there dawned upon people the awareness of a great working community, but the fruits of their labor benefitted only some individual workers and in all sorts of arbitrary and unjust ways. But now an order is emerging in which people work together for a common goal, no longer against each other but for each other, an order in which they unite in a new type of battle to meet the needs of material existence that before this had been too great for them, an order in which only one kind of competition exists—the competition of diligence and faithfulness in work.

Now that we have presented in broad outline the two ethical imperatives of the gospel as they relate to the economic order, let us place the economic order in the light of its highest religious goals. Like everything that is earthly, the economic order must serve God and glorify him. Let us ask ourselves if the order whose ethical *telos* we have now identified realizes these imperatives better than capitalism does, and also whether it comes closer to meeting the religious goal of our work — namely, the goal of a life of service to God. To do so it would have to restore and better realize three things upon which the existence of humanity primarily depends: work, the distribution of earthly goods, and the basic interpretation of the meaning of life.

Work! The worker is often accused of not working willingly and faithfully. Sometimes this may be true, but in such cases, it seems to me, it is often quite natural. How can anyone enjoy doing meaningless work? It is to his credit when he suffers under it. He is too good for it. In any case, such rebukes do not eliminate the evil. We must get at the roots of it. We have to find another relationship between man and his work. In many people's judgment we will not be able to eliminate mechanical work entirely, since it is closely tied to modern technology, but we can ennoble even this work by removing to the greatest possible degree its bad reputation as being just a way to make a living and by making the worker a full member of a democratic community of work and giving him all the rights and responsibilities thereof. A more heartfelt joy in one's work will then emerge.

In connection with this particular point, one often hears objections to a different moral approach to the economic order.

It is said that if the consideration of wages or profits falls more into the background, then all initiative, all inventiveness, all zeal to work will end. Self-interest is presumed to be the only lever that manages to move a sluggish humanity to action. Yet despite the fact that this objection occurs to all sensible people, it is nevertheless a false charge against human nature. I want to ask all who are gathered here, "Does concern about your income play any role in determining the zeal with which you do your duty? Are there not people in all positions, both men and women, who devote themselves body and soul to a cause without thinking of income?" There is a double motivation in people that is much stronger than the desire for gain: a drive for honor and an appetite for work. Just take away from people the yoke of having to think of wages and you will see how their nobler powers will develop, however slowly at first. Trust them to do their best, and they will do it. Nothing great has ever been achieved through the desire for profit. As long as man is degraded, he will naturally remain degraded; his work must be made honorable in order to elevate him. In keeping with God's will, work should surely entail more than earning money; it should entail the imitation of God, the confirmation of man's creation in God's image. All of this is said naturally with the assumption that in every society the dictum "He who does not work shall not eat" is valid. We do not argue for laziness but for a deeper meaning of work. We are not offering a postulate for today or tomorrow but searching for a principle to guide our evaluation and improvement of working conditions.

It is a similar case with the distribution of earthly goods. Until now there has never been a wholesome division. On one side there is a surplus, and on the other there is a shortage of even the elementary goods. On one side there are villas with huge gardens lived in only a few months a year, and on the other side there are tenement houses and dark, overcrowded hovels. There is unrestrained consumption here, and hot desire for denied goods there. Both these extremes—the great wealth and the great need—can and must end, although it is not necessary to bring about an absolute equality in property. The earth produces enough goods for all people to be satisfied. The table of the Lord is richly set for all his children. It was left to a Protestant clergyman (naturally I mean Malthus) to express the God-forsaken opposite view. It is simply a matter of obedience to God's commands. All can receive their daily bread; more is not necessary.

Under certain circumstances, however, bread becomes spirit. When the unspeakable burden of the battle for bread is someday lifted from the soul of mankind, then greatness and loveliness, sublimity and spirituality will sprout like the green corn that has long been yearning for the sun. Oh how freely we would be able to breathe if Mammonism no longer pressed us down! What new vistas would open up! It is true that until now the relationship of one person to another has been determined by money more than we have realized. In all the pores of the body of society there is gold dust, and everything that is noble within the body groans under this spell. Art, education, science—and yes, one might even say religion—are the privilege of but a few. A great cleavage cuts through our intellectual life. Our culture is terribly torn. There is no intellectual community anymore. Nevertheless, a time will come when man will relate to man on the basis of common humanity, and then a new culture will develop on this new basis, the beauty of which we can only surmise. After man has gained again confidence in the spirit, and after he has found his soul and his brother, then he will also find God. For God and man belong together.

At this point, our hope reaches its peak. The social movement reveals itself as the true way to God for our race. In a world where soul has capitulated to matter and where personality has capitulated to mechanism, how can anyone believe in a reasonable goal, in a wise and kind Providence, in an infinite Being as the foundation of the world, or in the eternal value of the soul? It has been more natural to perceive the world as a soulless machine and believe in blind rules of natural law than in a purposeful personal Providence. Yes, under the tremendous pressure of a materialistic culture, it has been difficult to believe in God and in the soul. But as soon as the personality of the self and of the other, of the soul and the spirit, once again come into their own, they will seek and find on their own their roots and their citizenship in a kingdom of personal spirits under a personal God. How should a modern proletarian, degraded by the machine, made into a number, tossed to and fro by the maelstrom of an unreasonable and heartless economic system—how should he believe in a providential God of wisdom and love? Now, however, it is beginning to dawn on him: God meets him again in hope and help.

It seems to me that it is not difficult for eyes that are at all accustomed to seeing God's action to perceive his work in the movement of these times. We had gone so far that without such an intervention by God our faith in him and in man might have faded away. We had come to an end of human understanding. We looked at this modern world with its appearance of culture and we saw its distance from God, its alienation and its ugliness. We saw the proletarian masses in factories and tenement houses live unhappy, empty lives. We saw the family, piety, and morality decay. Everything beautiful in life, everything noble in human existence seemed to have become a myth. There was charity, of course, but precisely those who wanted to help saw that charitable attempts to eliminate ever-growing evil resembled efforts to empty a swamp that was filling up with ever faster flowing water. Then God himself took action. An earthquake shook the foundations of society, and minds awoke from philistinism, from hedonism, from satiation with the world, from the temple of Mammon worship and of culture deification. A new spirit emerged, a fear of God, a search for deeper meaning in life. All those believers in God and man who wandered through the wilderness parched with thirst raised up their heads and cried "Maranatha." The poor proletariat listened. "The people who sat in darkness have seen a great light, and for those who sat in the region and shadow of death light has dawned" (Matt. 4:16; see 4:12–17). Thus for them also hope appeared. The lifeless came to life (Ezek. 37); they began to organize.

For all who can see clearly, the organization presents a striking example of divine work that is accomplished before our very eyes. Who was supposed to help these multitudes separated from the soil, alienated from ecclesiastical, political, and social communities, and also unfulfilled in their work? Then came the movement—the political organization, the labor union, the cooperative. They were the rescuers. They made the workers members of a reputable community and brought them under the discipline of the community. They filled them with a new ethos, with a sense of responsibility, with self-respect and self-confidence. The workers now amounted to something. Their minds were filled with great thoughts and their hearts with bright hope. At first only an elite was stirred, but then larger and larger circles. The men who lead these workers' organizations are performing perhaps the most important task that can be performed now. They are often people who have done heavy industrial work during the day, and then they spend their evenings advising the union, handling accounts, and making speeches while some prosperous citizens sit by their drinks and complain about the laziness and the overindulgence of the workers. How much patience this work demands, how much ingratitude it incurs—often from those whom they serve! These men stand in the service of God, even when they deny him. Whoever disputes the right of the organization is wrong. The unorganized strikebreaker, however, does not deserve the respect that he is getting nowadays in certain quarters, even if in certain cases he may deserve a certain amount of sympathy. The cooperative movement is often based on ethical ideals —

and yes, even on religious ideals — that are seen as standing in
close relation to the gospel, and justifiably so.

Therefore I think that we who believe in the gospel may
follow this whole development with deep joy and reverent
anticipation. We too may hope, and hoping means living. We see
before us some high — distant, to be sure — but yet realizable
goals. We have suffered and dare now believe that we are freed
from captivity. We can work again with confidence. We now see
a chance that the sorely tried family is again being built up on
new foundations, that the housing and food situation is improv-
ing, that having children is once again recognized as a blessing.
There is hope that enemies that once seemed unconquerable,
such as alcohol and prostitution, can yet be overcome because
the growing awareness of human rights and human worth will
someday not tolerate them. The increased economic indepen-
dence of women, purchased through such misery, will serve
more and more as a dam against the horrible enormity of vice.
The joy of living will take on nobler forms.

We are thinking here, and justly so, not only of the industrial workers but also of farmers. At this point, we cannot
outline any agricultural program. Everyone who understands
the conditions of our peasant class knows that there is a need for
a release from its burdens. The social problems are present in
rural areas as much as in the cities, only in a different form.
Mortgage reforms and cooperatives will no doubt be the two
pillars upon which the help for the rural areas will have to be
built. But I cannot speak about it further, other than to express
the conviction that this new movement will prove to be a
blessing also for the peasant class. It will be good for the farmers
to get away from the stagnation, the self-centered narrowness,
the interest in piling up money (things that they have been
accused of). The economic development will give them a push
from the old into a new alliance.

Our hope is not for just one class but for all. As we have
stated repeatedly, those classes that gain the most economically
out of the present order also suffer—inwardly, often only
half-knowingly, but sometimes very consciously and intensely.
They should also be helped, even if it is painful for them, even if
it is against their will. Our hope embraces all nations. Should not
the new spirit that we sense, await, and encourage, gradually
affect the relationships among nations to the extent that world
peace would no longer appear to be a dream of childish and
naive minds? After the spirit of solidarity and the respect for the
sacredness of humanity have brought about changes in the
relationships within individual nations, they will not stop at the

borders. All individual manifestations of the social struggle point, as we have seen, to a deeper unity in a spiritual movement that includes all mankind. Mankind wants to take a step upward toward the goals given and promised by God.

What we have been considering is an act in the drama of the humanizing of mankind, whose value we do not quite realize yet. The soul battles against things — the personality against chaos, the will against fate. Mechanism seemed to have become powerful. People were bent mournfully under the yoke of alien powers. Material conditions, an impersonal culture, and competition had become seemingly unconquerable masters. Then in a storm appeared God, a personal Spirit who wanted to create Kingdom of personal spirits. He came to knock down idols from their pedestals, to save people from the curse of materialism and mechanism, to liberate them from the slavery to Mammon and lethargy into the light of a human and moral existence, into the freedom of the children of God. It is an act of creation that we are witnessing. Human souls are reaching upward, toward the sunlight and toward new goals; they are shaken, compelled by built-in inner longings, but they are doing it because he, the Creator and Father, beckons and calls.

IV

There are certain specific questions that must be dealt with. Is Switzerland not ahead of other countries in its provisions for workers? No, Germany and England are more advanced. Is the right to strike something that a Christian should support? Yes, it is an essential instrument for social improvement. A Christian should enter into it, however, without class hatred. He should not approve every strike. Revolutionary movements can get carried to extremes. Does religious socialism expect the social movement to bring heaven to earth? No, after social reform there will be new sources of conflict and difficulty. But this earth can be made much better. One does not have to be a utopian to believe it. It is terrible to see Christians refuse to try to improve society on the grounds that it is too evil or altogether hopeless. The yeast belongs in the dough; it should not be kept away from it. A loving action toward a neighbor will help the world see what it means to believe in a great and all-powerful God.

V

Opponents of socialism charge that it eliminates private property and personal freedom. This is not true. Small private property, especially on the land, will be retained, even expanded. Only certain large concerns will be nationalized. Freedom is not identified with one economic system. There are limits to freedom under capitalism. The freedom of the full expression of one's individuality can be realized in socialism. People argue against cooperation with the workers' movement because it is rough, crude, and materialistic. The middle class need not be so self-righteous; it commits the same sins. Furthermore, many of the failings of the working class are the result of what society has done. The workers' embrace of materialistic philosophy is due partly to the church's failure to take material needs seriously. We need to bring Christian influence into the movement. Socialism need not be materialistic.

VI

The class division in society should be a source of great concern to pastors. They can do something about it. First of all, they must understand the whole situation: not only the economic facts, but also the moral and religious difficulties inherent in the social crisis. Pastors can make a great contribution to bringing about the ethical and religious foundation of the new order. It would be great if people were to flee the church not just because it is preaching the "same old stuff" but because it is preaching the truth — even if the truth hurts. Then we pastors could talk with workers again. Then they would listen.

VII

What is needed is a religious rebirth. A renewal of the church in the near future is unlikely. The church is a middle-class church. It is a preachers' church. It is not a community. Someday it must again become a Spirit-guided community.

To summarize: We have tried to show that a radical change of the present society is a consequence of following the teachings of Jesus. But for the full realization of that change we need persons in whom these teachings are embodied. Genuine change will come about not by a change of society alone; a radical renewal of the spirit is also required. "Social change can topple capitalism and with it Mammonism, but not necessarily selfishness and greed; it can bring about a fairer distribution of the earth's goods, but still not satisfy the souls of men; it can link people together socially but not unite them in the deepest sense." Social change and religious reform need each other.

In 1907 Ragaz delivered an address at a conference in Boston and traveled through parts of America. His journal records of his impressions (fragments of which are presented here) were published posthumously in his autobiography, Mein Weg (vol. 1, pp. 255–88). Ragaz admired American freedom and equality, the active role of women in public life, and the free churches (i.e., churches independent of the state), but was appalled by some sights, such as the contrast between the housing of whites and blacks in Washington, D.C. He was deeply moved by his visit to Plymouth, Massachusetts.

TRIP TO AMERICA

In the subway and in the train we came upon a thoroughly un-European democratic conduct. There was no noticeable class difference. Even if there was some small difference in dress, there was none in bearing. The maid was just as self-confident as the lady from Fifth Avenue, and the butcher's apprentice was as proud as the millionaire who perhaps sat next to him....

This primordial democratic way of life struck me as soon as I stepped on the soil of the New World. It was the atmosphere in which I moved. It was unlike our country, where the question of whether a man has money or not determines his value, where consciously or unconsciously human relationships are ruled by monetary evaluation. The dollar, which according to the self-righteous presuppositions of those who don't know anything about it rules all life over there, made less of an imprint on the land than did the taler or hundred franc bill in our country. Not that it doesn't play a role, but it does so much more as a playing chip than as a measure of social worth; a man knows how rich he is, but he also knows that this does not determine his total worth. Money is not gripped as tightly in the hand there as it is here. If a person loses a fortune overnight, he does not lose honor and life's happiness; he just sets himself to the task of getting it back. Work, including manual labor, is not considered degrading. It means more than money. And more easily than here, people open their hands to give, often quite generously.

There is a contradiction, however, between this primordial democratic, truly human outlook and an element that a European finds utterly offensive: the status of the black American. Normally he is not mistreated, but he is considered second-class. And it would not suit him at all if we tried to treat him different from the way to which he is accustomed. That hit us rather hard. It made a strong impression upon us to see even in Washington a street where on one side were the very neat villas of the whites and on the other side the primitive and dirty shacks of the blacks....

During our visit in Tarrytown Mr. Weeks gave us a stimulating book written by Rauschenbusch, the first book by him we had seen, and this introduced us to him and his way of thinking....

Still more important was an excursion, or should I call it a pilgrimage, to Plymouth, the place where in 1620 the Mayflower landed, carrying the Pilgrim forefathers. They point out the rock in the bay upon which the Pilgrims threw their anchor. Above it still stands the little old church, and in the cemetery next to it are the sunken graves of those male and female pioneers. It is, from a spiritual point of view, the place with the widest vista I have experienced on earth. The sight of the ocean stirs my soul deeply at any time, but here my soul's deepest longing broke forth, and I wished ardently to be allowed, like those Pilgrim fathers, to serve God in freedom. Those hours stimulated a deep revolutionary impulse for my later life....

This American trip, like the later trip to England, brought about a close relationship with the Anglo-Saxon world and proved to have a decisive significance for my thinking and acting. Without them the story of my life would be incomplete.

In 1908, at the close of his ministry in Basel, Ragaz
delivered a farewell sermon, expressing in it his
belief in the Kingdom and his "theology of hope":
"God is not behind us but before us." One's view
should not be directed toward the past, he said, but
toward the present and the future. This sermon
appears in the collection Dein Reich Komme (vol. 2,
pp. 295–306).

THY KINGDOM COME

Dear congregation,

As I NOW THINK of what I had in view during all of the time I
worked with you... I find it best expressed in the petition Jesus
gave his disciples when he taught them to pray "Thy Kingdom
come."

This phrase, dear congregation, is, so to speak, the banner
that will be carried in the march of the cause of Jesus, or shall we
say the cause of mankind. It shows us that the cause of Jesus
provides above all a great hope, that it does not look backward but
rather forward, that it is something that still has not been realized,
that is still to come. Like others, I too have been caught up in the
forward march of the cause of Jesus. As one who hopes, yearns,
looks forward, I have spoken, worked, fought, suffered, rejoiced.
Hope and future I have proclaimed to you. Perhaps I may briefly
point out how it happened that this hopeful characteristic of the
gospel became clear to me, that this forward-pointing banner
came to be mine.

When six and a half years ago I preached my first sermon in
this pulpit, I described to you how with great pains I sought to
find the way to God and how I believed that I had found him.
Today I would like to say that what I have experienced and done
since then is only the continuation of the earlier experience and of
the confession of faith made at that time. To the petition "God, let
us find thee" there belongs the other one, "Thy kingdom come."
The first part of my life was filled with the struggle for God. That
was the content of my life, the soul of my soul, my misery and my
bliss. To confess this to you is certainly neither immodest nor
rude, for I would not have had the right to speak about God from
the pulpit if I had not been a God-seeker myself. It is what I am
still and what I shall remain. None of us dare give up the struggle

18

for God. But in my case, the seeking was rewarded by finding. Here, however, there occurred a further development that affected both me and you. If a man has found God, then he feels irresistibly impelled to see him in real life. He wants to recognize his rule in all that exists in his own life and in the life of the world. It becomes his great desire, and the more he seizes God, or, more accurately, the more God seizes him—the more it becomes his passion that the world may belong to God, that it may become his Kingdom. In us, the children of the Reformed Church in whom still dwells a trace of the spirit of Zwingli and Calvin, there lives (in some people more, in others less) the feeling that the will of the great and holy God should be embodied in a sanctified world. So we look into the world in order to find God's presence, God's Kingdom therein. And we do find traces of it everywhere. Yet what we see does not satisfy us. Besides the clear ways of God we see a jungle of problems; besides the light of the goodness that comes from him, the Good One, and witnesses to him, we see the horrible shadows of evil. What are we to say? On the one hand there is the great, holy God, the father of justice and love, and on the other hand there is an imperfect, dark world filled with much that is ungodly. Which will prove to be right?

In this clash the flame of hope flares up: God will prove to be right—but it is the coming God that will prove to be right. God's creation is not yet finished; his last word has by no means been spoken. What we see now is a plan, a preliminary sketch. Ahead of us lies the unfolding, the completion. Something great and glorious awaits us. God goes before us, a restlessly working God, coaxing us onward, supporting us, sometimes working on us in silence, sometimes tempestuously shaking us out of our sensuousness and earthly bondage, out of our spiritual indolence and spiritual slavery, out of our sin and affliction, into the freedom and glory of the children of God.

This is the message about the living God, which is intended to change all of our religious thinking and acting. Many, indeed most of us who believe in God, had fallen into three errors. First of all, to put it briefly, we apprehended God too theoretically. We labored hard to understand the theory, to accept it as true, but still it didn't quite ring true. Or—and this was the second erroneous path—if he was more than a theory, he nevertheless remained too much a God of the past. He had formerly revealed himself through Moses, the prophets, and Jesus, but that was it. To be sure, he spoke to us through nature, through our conscience, through our life experience, but we took his creative and revelatory work to be essentially finished. Thus—and this was our third error—we stood helpless before the evil of the world. To be sure, we knew that somehow evil too must serve the good, and yet there was much that we didn't quite understand, and this lack of understanding depressed us. We thought that creation was finished and that all that remained was hope for the next life. We deceived ourselves in this way and did not rejoice about God. But now a bright light has illuminated us. God's work with the world and with us is not done. He has just begun. He is in the middle of his work. Everything, including ourselves, is in a state of becoming. He worked in the past, he awakened life and spirit on this planet, and finally he formed the human being, his child. He spoke through prophets of all kinds. At the turning point in time he let shine the fullness of his love and life in Jesus Christ and let that light stream into our human world. At that time the outline of his Kingdom became clear. But he didn't give a law. He didn't reveal a system or dogma. Nor did he found a church. Rather, he established the beginning of a life that is to go on, that is to unfold and become purer and richer.

The goal is fixed; it has been revealed in which direction mankind should move. Our destiny is clear. But he, the living God, has continued working, building, right up to now, and he keeps striding on into the future. Historical movements are the work of his hands; he rules in them. He carries out what has been planned within us and within the world, fulfills promises, turns shadows into light. He leads yearning mankind upward to the height of true humanity befitting the children of God, just as he leads each yearning human being to his or her own great and personal goal. All the bright and holy things that we dream about will someday become reality — not in exactly the same form we dream about them, but in an even greater and more beautiful form. God goes before us. We have a God who is not just a system, a theory, a past history, but a God who works constantly, a God of the present, of the future, a God who gives to us too a future and a hope. Let no one despair. God still has much to say to each of us!

This is what I would like to say to you in this farewell hour. Continue to look forward, to stride forward, to be more and more filled with hope. We cannot hope enough, for we have a great God. To know that is happiness and life. It is wonderful to see God working in one's life and in the life of the world, to sense him in the movements of the time, to follow him into the future; this makes the world, history, one's own life meaningful. This is a wealth that surpasses and transcends all the poverty of individual existence. I am thankful above all to this city, because it was not until I came here that my hope came into full bloom, like a flower in spring. Here despite the storms and the need I have become rich and happy again, and I wish each of you something of this spring that has its source in the faith in the living God. But then what is it that we hope for?

Dear congregation! Jesus has announced God's reign on earth. This reign is to come about through the realization of God's will on earth as in heaven. God's life and God's love are to stream into the world. In this way redemption is to come. That is the central message of the good news. Redemption means liberation. We are to be freed from everything that holds us in its grip; we—that is, mankind, and in it each one of us as an individual—are to become what we were meant to be. We are to become free children of God, free from guilt, free from hate, free from the tyranny of the world and of death, free from service to Mammon, free from self-service; we are to breathe freely in the freedom of God and become united in a Kingdom of freedom, purity, justice, and love. A liberated world, a world that belongs to God is Jesus' goal just as it is the goal of all other men of God. He has made it known not only in word but also in his person, his life, his death, and his victory. And we sense that this liberation is something that is only beginning to be realized. But we yearn for it. And that, it seems to me, is the meaning of the religious movement of our time. We would like to see the old, great promises of redemption become a reality; we would like the word to become flesh everywhere among us just as it became flesh in Jesus. Wherever we look today, be it in the field of education or art or any other area of human endeavor, everywhere there is striving and longing to get away from inauthentic forms, spiritless stereotypes, to find life, to serve life, to allow the soul to find its rightful place in relation to things, to educate people, to draw them out, to free them. In short, we thirst for life, truth, reality.

It is precisely the purpose of the religious movement that seizes and stirs us to give us these things. It wants more reality, more life. It fights therefore against everything that is simply form, that has merely the appearance of life. That is why we are critical of the church, of our religious conditions, of our Christianity, of our morals, and of our social order. We criticize out of hunger for the true life inspired by God, out of thirst for the living God. We want to experience something of the freedom of God's children and of brotherhood. We would like to see something of redemption also out in the world, in the world of material things, in work, trade, and industry, in the way individuals and nations live together, and we wish that here, too, the highest law would not be power and violence and brutality but rather the law of God that manifests itself in just and kind humaneness.

It is here that the religious movement becomes united with

the social movement. To find this union has been the central search of my soul. It has dominated my speaking and my working. In this pursuit I have experienced battle and storm, hatred and anger, but also joy and awakening, love and enthusiasm. May I in this hour briefly mention something about it? I sincerely wish that many people would understand how for me and for many others social volition is bound up with religious faith. Our social hopes and work are simply results of the desire that God might become real in everything.

If God is the Father, if he is the God of love, then we his children are brothers, mankind is a family, and the law of solidarity that is based on a unifying God and on the law of service that forms the kernel of the gospel should rule among us. In politics, trade, and industry, solidarity, mutual effort, and service should replace bitter war. These, too, must be freed from hatred, from service to Mammon, and from egoism and must become a service to God—and thus also a service to man. We cannot give up this goal, so long as we believe in the teachings of Jesus, in the Kingdom of God which is also for this earth. Since I believe in it, I have seized this goal with all my soul. I do not know how long it will take until we get closer to it, nor by what particular ways it will one day be reached, but I believe in the goal. And since I believe in the living God who rules over the various movements in history, I also see him in the social movement. He exhorts and calls us through it. It discloses to us the highest goals of mankind revealed to us by Jesus—and it does so even in the midst of storm and chaos. I participate in it in fear and hope, because I want to walk with the living God.

I am also drawn by a strong love for people, especially the working people. God gave this love to me. I haven't really done anything; I was obligated. Woe to me if I hadn't obeyed. Something compels, forces me to show the worker that I understand him, that I would like to do justly by him, that I see the greater spiritual goals that overshadow his economic struggle which he himself often does not recognize. I would like to serve him with my heart, with my knowledge and understanding. I would like to show him that the great promises of God's Kingdom are there for him if he can understand his struggle correctly. The battle will be blessed and its goal will be reached only if the thoughts of brotherhood and service are asserted; we will be redeemed only if in the struggle and need the springs of God pour out upon us.

Thus for me religious and social movements belong together. Out of the natural craving of the heart, but also out of the desire to fulfill the will of God and Christ, I have worked with much

spiritual anguish and have gone through struggles of belief in this
place. Each contact with God and Christ drives me to my
brothers. One serves God the Father through service to men, his
children: that is the central teaching of the gospel. He will always
reveal himself more clearly. Religion and socialism flow together
in him. But one serves God above all when one serves the least of
Jesus' brethren. The love of God yearns to shine into the lowly
places so that they should become bright. It shines today in
innumerable hearts. The social movement is, after all, not just a
workers' movement; it is an upward movement of the people who
are held down. It is the year of the Lord for the oppressed and the
disadvantaged of all sorts. Do you not see how hearts everywhere
are eager to help, to rescue, to take care of those who live in
darkness and neglect? That is God's action. The depths are
illuminated by the sun of redemption. Yes, the depths! But the
heights, too, are more joyous when the depths are liberated.
Redemption is for everyone; salvation comes to each one.

The redemption that is promised to us will not be solely
economic. No, it will go out from the Center and return to the
Center. If I were to summarize in two words what we need and
what I desire for most of us, I would say it is *freedom* and *unity*
that we need....

God is the basis of unity among people. Through him people
learn to understand one another. Here is the spring of genuine
freedom, for when people understand and respect each other
they become free. Here is also the only religious freedom
available. We argue about freedom as Catholics and Protestants,
Positivists and Reformers, believers and freethinkers, or whatever we want to call ourselves. We do not realize freedom by
rejecting this or that dogma, however, or by creating this or that
liberal institution, but rather by allowing our hearts to become
great and free in God's greatness and freedom....

Let us have great thoughts and remain steadfast, and above
all let us not shy away from suffering. Let us stride forward with
the living God as living persons, never wavering, never giving up
in the long run. Let us try, each in his own place, to realize
something of our yearning for the Kingdom of God and his
righteousness, to gather some of its strength in us and to share it.
We part, but our hearts should not be filled with pains of parting,
but rather with holy joy for God's cause. Let all our pain, all our
gratitude, all our hope be expressed in the petition "Thy Kingdom
Come!"

Amen.

PART II

The Kingdom and Violence 1914–1932

Ragaz viewed World War I as a judgment of God upon the churches as well as upon society. All that he found negative in the churches he labeled "religion." In this meditation, written in 1917, his critique is clearly expressed. It originally appeared in Weltreich, Religion und Gottesherrschaft *(vol. 1, pp. 141–58).*

NOT RELIGION BUT THE KINGDOM OF GOD

OUT OF THE BATTLE BETWEEN THE DARKNESS of a passing night and the sunlight of a new creation dawning over the existing chaos, there arises our one hope: Christ and his Kingdom. "The old is past; see how all has become new." Parties, trends, churches, various types of Christianity are overthrown and fall. They no longer enjoy the confidence of strong souls. Who still believes that they can really help and save? From God, out of the depth of God-seized souls, there has to come a new being and thereby the strength for the birth of a new world of the future. This new world, the Kingdom of God, is different from the other kingdom that has usurped its place under the pretense of being the Kingdom of God itself. This other kingdom is so strong that it obscures the view into the nature of the genuine Kingdom of God. It even persists in concealing Jesus. We must try to free Jesus and his cause from the obscurities and distortions that have surrounded him so that the free and deep spirits who are now on the way to God might know what we are talking about. Let us repeat for their sake a few things that have often been said before. All independent spirits, of course, see these things and express them in their own way, but we would do well to look at them in a cohesive context rather than in the confusion of various partial passing references.

First of all, it needs to be said once again that the Kingdom of God is not a religion, but rather its opposite. In this sentence lies a tremendous amount of yet unrecognized truth, which, when it once comes to light, can bring about a great revolution, a much greater one than the Russian Revolution — the greatest revolution imaginable and possible. It is a truth that makes the whole world explode. All the great revolutions of the past have come out of it.

The Kingdom of God is no religion but rather the abolishment of all religion. For many people this must be the most shocking thing that can be said, for from time immemorial people have embraced in the word *religion* everything that their souls conceive as most holy. Is it not the word that brings sunshine to our souls? No matter how often it is misused, it nevertheless represents for the pious soul the highest possession: communion of the soul with God. Do we want to impugn this treasure of the soul, this absolutely holiest possession, by speaking out against religion? Is it not just a question of a word, and would it not be better to let a word that is so precious to so many people stand rather than create terrible misunderstandings through questioning it? In questioning it we run the risk of appearing to be atheists, blasphemers, destroyers of all that is holy.

And yet, we cannot do otherwise. For here two worlds separate. We are dealing with one of the basic truths, one of the basic decisions.

What do we usually understand by the word *religion?* Certainly not the communion of the soul with God, but something else. More often than not, a person sees in the word *religion* a certain spiritual structure that can easily be described. Included in it is a doctrine — a doctrine about God and divine things, a holy doctrine. Included in it are also certain practices and customs, exercises and institutions. Above all, included in it is what is called "worship," or "cult," and also some kind of community that gathers around this doctrine and worship. In addition, there is some kind of organization that arranges this worship, regulates this community, transmits the professed truth to the coming generations and to those outside the community. There has to be some kind of formulated confession of faith, even if it takes the freest form. And there will be a certain separation from other religions.

In general, it is a characteristic of religion that in this fashion it creates its own image. It becomes a kingdom for itself. It separates itself from morality, art, science, politics. Naturally, it will try to come into contact with these areas of life to dominate or penetrate them, but basically it remains something that has an identity of its own, and it is often believed that the more it guards itself against mixing with the world, the more genuine and sincere it is.

Let us add that vital religion is not just a dogma or a ritual or an organization but above all a matter of feeling, disposition, and sentiment. It is a whole world of dispositions, an unending symphony of sentiments. The scale of religious feelings reaches from the deepest hell to the highest heaven. All jubilation and all agony, all light and all darkness that inhabit the infinite reaches of the human soul find their strongest and fullest expression in religion. A large part of religious life has to do with the cultivation of these feelings. Their strength and fullness pass as a measure of the worth of one's religiousness.

This, then, is what is normally understood by religion. This is what is loved or hated, cultivated or destroyed as religion. Is that not so?

And now let us note that what Jesus wants is something quite different, virtually the opposite. We would have to say that already about Israel. What is called the religion of Israel is in fact no religion. At any rate, this is true of the kernel and basic purpose of Old Testament faith. To call it a religion is to misjudge and distort it. It is precisely the uniqueness of Israel that it seeks to do something unlike what the heathen religions do. Moses wanted no religion, and the battle of the prophets was a battle *against* religion. What did they want then? Not a religion, but rather a Kingdom—the Kingdom of God and people, a world of justice and goodness. In the name of God they stood against the temple and the priests for the lordship of God himself.

Jesus also stands in this line: he follows it to the end. Not only does he not bring a new religion, he does not bring any religion at all. One can't make this fact clear enough. He does not want a religion, but rather a Kingdom, a new creation, a new world. He wants God, the people, the brother, a new justice, the liberation of the world from fear and sensuality, from Mammonism, from despair, from death—and from religion. The old era is to pass and a new one is to come. We cannot think realistically enough about the cause of Jesus. A Catholic church teacher says that the Catholic Church is not invisible (as Protestants have said of the true church), but rather as visible and tangible as the kingdom of France or the republic of Venice, and that is precisely how Jesus understood the Kingdom of God. It is a Kingdom as tangible and visible as the Roman Empire, even though in its basic nature it is the exact opposite of it: as is self-evident, despite all its realness, it is marked by immense spirituality. What Jesus wants is a world order based on God, not a religion.

This becomes apparent as soon as we take off the religious glasses through which we look at his message and his work. There is no religious dogma in it. Again and again it has been a puzzle to theologians and philosophers that Jesus paid so little attention to putting his teachings into specific forms in order to ensure their correct interpretation for all time, for which purpose a precise tradition and a written record would have been necessary. His lack of concern on this point appears to us to be unbelievably great, almost as if — let's face it — he were half-hearted about his message. Apparently for Jesus the primary concern is not a dogma about God; indeed, we seem to feel distinctly that he evades it and may even be brushing it off with a smile. His God is so immensely understandable and, despite all the paradoxes of his being, so self-evident. Every human mind can understand him without trouble as soon as these veils have been removed that human wisdom, and especially religion, have put on him. What Jesus does is primarily this: with a firm hand he removes these veils and shows God in such a way that man can understand him right away. Thus the God of Jesus has something so inexplicably enlightening, so radiantly—yes, more than radiantly clear — and sweet about him that practically no human soul can say no to him.

But one doesn't need a religion to serve this God. One serves him by serving men. Let us consider certain obvious truths that are nonetheless of enormous importance. Nowhere does Jesus give instruction regarding any special practices or works. With a smile he rejects fasting as a religious law, though on the other hand he does not forbid or condemn it. Nor does he urge people to pray — or at any rate not in the way that we usually understand it. On the contrary, he recommends moderation; only a few great petitions should fill the hearts of the disciples (and these should be as natural as breathing), and should all pertain to the coming of the Kingdom. One shouldn't pray just for prayer's sake, in order to be pious and pleasing to God, or for the sake of religious practices or mood, but rather as a co-worker and fellow combatant with God. In this sense alone Jesus urges one to make courageous, even impudent petitions. Likewise, he does not establish a worship service — there is no trace of it. He does go to the synagogue on the Sabbath day, but not to "build up" the synagogue. Rather, the synagogue is the place where Israel's hopes are still represented; it is a community gathering, a place where the Kingdom of God is discussed in some way, even though it is done under the cloak of religion. The Sabbath he views in the same way, in that he basically stands above it. Nor do we find anywhere any instructions on how to cultivate a pious disposition or religious sincerity. There is no mysticism, no forced talk about God. One can say, using Gottfried Keller's words, that his God beams with worldliness.

As he reveals himself in everyday life, so he is served in everyday life.

In short, it is a plain truth and yet a great paradox: Jesus does not have the slightest interest in making people pious. He does not want any religious people. His sphere is not religion. What he wants is not some mystical power cut off from the rest of life; he does not want any separation at all. He does not draw lines of demarcation among religions, but rather the opposite: he tears down religious barriers, as the parable of the Good Samaritan—this terribly revolutionary word—shows. There is no confession in the sense of a creed. Not even the Lord's Prayer constitutes such a thing. In Jesus' sense a confession is simply a faithful stand taken for God's and Jesus' cause. In short, there is nowhere a temple atmosphere, a church atmosphere, be it ever so sacred, or a mystical twilight; instead, everywhere there is God's free sky and God's fresh air. There is nowhere anything artistic, extravagant, or man-made, but rather something simple, natural, genuine, healthy, clear as daylight, very human and very divine.

So very human and so very divine! We had better say so very human *because* so very divine — for this is actually the remarkable thing: here, where religion stops, we have the deep awareness of being with God. Religion ends *because* God is present. Everything is earthly *because* God has been seen in stark reality. Wherever one needs that holy, secluded, special world that is called religion, there one cannot be sure that God is near, there one needs a substitute — namely, religion. Where God is a self-evident, supremely clear, all-penetrating reality, there he can be seen in all things, can be felt in all things, can be honored in all things, can be served in all things. The world is truly his temple; therefore the special temple falls by the wayside. All people automatically become priests; therefore a special priesthood is not needed. All days become holy; therefore special holy days are not needed. Every deed becomes an act of worship; therefore worship services are no longer needed. Everything becomes holy; therefore nothing remains that is specially holy or unholy. Religion tumbles before God.

That is the revolution of Jesus, the immeasurable, still little-understood revolution. To be sure, the religion of his time understood it, and the result was the cross. Many more crosses will be raised before it is clearly understood. But precisely here lies the endless drawing power of Jesus for all human souls, pious and "godless," Christian and heathen: in the way in which he has brought God and man together, in the fact that he does not teach religion, that he does not bind anyone to a creed but

rather opens a world, the world of people and the world of God
—but of the God who is real, who belongs to people, whom each
human soul qua soul greets, whom man seeks and cannot do
without. Religion turns many souls away, but the Kingdom of
God attracts all even if it doesn't win all.

Now we want to return to religion and try to examine its
nature more fully. Why do we want to supplant religion with the
Kingdom of God?

Religion is without doubt the greatest creation of the human
spirit. Indeed, it is religion that distinguishes a human from an
animal, that elevates him high above an animal, that makes him a
new being, a new creature. Religion comprises the innermost
depth of human history; it is the creator of culture, the Sunday of
the world. How many great things have been done in its name!
What a world of quiet splendor is contained in the hidden life of
the soul with God! Should this all be questioned and destroyed?

No, we do not want to question or destroy it by any means.
We never question or destroy anything that is truly holy. God
forbid! But there are a number of unpleasant truths that we must
assert.

First, we have just stated that religion is by far the greatest
creation of the human spirit. In this highest praise of religion we
have immediately distinguished between religion and the Kingdom of God. A creation of the human spirit! That is indeed what
religion is. That is its glory, but also its limitation. From this
basic fact several others can be derived.

Religion is a creation of the human *psyche*. Thus it shares in
the characteristics of the human soul, whose offspring it is. It
will manifest its relationship to God, its divine nobility, but also
its fallen nature, its sensuality and forlornness: it can lift itself into
the suprahuman realm, but it can also sink to the subhuman
level. It may help the spirit express its highest striving, but it may
also merely bestow its luster and its sentimentality on the
physical side of man. It can provide us with a wonderful image,
but still not the slightest certainty that we are dealing with God
himself, for we remain completely in the realm of the human.
Human customs, human thoughts, human sentiments are no
guarantee whatsoever that God is involved. One can have much
religion and still be far from God; one can in fact be wholly
godless.

We talk of false religion, but we often fail to see that a false
religion can be a thoroughly genuine religion. It can be perfectly
honest, deeply felt, enthusiastic and exciting religion. It can well
up in passionate souls with a great psychic power. It can affect
others violently. In exceptional cases whole religions can be

established that have nothing to do with God, that are nil before God. Religion can be in essence only human fire. It can be mixed with open or hidden selfishness and love of power—and often is. It can turn into a strong deceit; yes, it can be a demonic lie. It can be the highest expression of man's titanism and reach to heaven, but even if it reaches to heaven it won't reach God—not the real God. He may overthrow this or that religious tower of Babel with a puff of his breath just as he overthrows the cultural Babel.

What, then, is religion other than the most enchanting expression of culture? In all times there have been great religious men who have been honored by many people but about whom it probably can be said that "the least in the Kingdom of Heaven are greater than they." There have been great religious revivals that were nothing more in the eyes of God than godlessness—even something worse than open godlessness. For religion is often nothing but a terrible fraud.

The real God transcends purely human images. He comes to man and unites himself with him, but he comes from above and changes him in that act. To be sure, he thereby makes man into a true human. He is the God of justice and love, from whom comes the Kingdom. It is there he rules, and there only. It is there he appears in man, always synonymous with simple human morality, with goodness, humility, freedom, purity of heart, trust, and above all in self-denial. The converse is true as well: where these virtues are, there is God, even if his name is not mentioned; and where they are not, there he is not, even if all walls echo his name. But it is an old feeling of true men of God that God despises nothing more than the empty use of his name, hates nothing more than religion. Why does God need religion? He does not demand religion, but rather faith and love. Religion is demanded by the gods; God demands that his will be done on earth for the good of men.

We cannot be sufficiently on guard when it comes to religion —in the name of God. We don't need religion; we need the Kingdom of God. Because of an inherited affliction we are still much too inclined to honor everything that looks like religion, to dote on religious words, religious enthusiasm, religious earnestness, and religious profundity. We must, however, definitely turn away from all this as from one of the great anaesthetizations of the human soul. We must become more and more distrustful of religion; we must keep an ever-stricter eye upon it. Again and again we must distinguish between religion and God. Religion is a human creation, often magnificent and wonderful, but just as often contaminated with everything that is inhumane and subhuman. But God is—God. He is the world of the Holy, the pure will of the Good. He is completely different from humans, distinguished from them qualitatively—and it is precisely this that makes him so human, so friendly to men, so liberating, so caring and attentive to men. We don't need religion. We need God.

Our second point is this: as we have seen, religion has the tendency to withdraw into itself, to form its own world. This is a fact the great and fateful implications of which we must examine. Perhaps we could express what we mean by saying that religion has a tendency to become something that is important for its own sake. One cannot have enough religion; therefore, one cultivates religion. One becomes terribly concerned about religious theory, the right dogma. One builds up the religious community to be as strong and as correct as possible and elevates it where possible to authority over all others. One puts much stress on a correct and enthusiastic worship. One generates within himself pious sentiments and believes that they please God, and one attends anxiously to their volatility. In doing so, one can easily conclude that the "purer" one's religion is, the less it has to do with the world and its affairs, the more valuable and more genuine it is. From such a view there emerges that kind of religious excess that chokes whole nations; from such a view there emerges the sort of religious activity that considers the building of one more chapel, the celebration of one more mass, the preaching of one more sermon to be a great achievement, that considers a gathering prefaced by a devotion to be a far more God-oriented enterprise than one that is not so prefaced. What always counts is the *form* of religion: where the form is present, there is the true seriousness and the true depth, there is God.

What is the fruit of this kind of thinking? In order to show what it is, we will refer to the observation just made about the matter of religious *form*—that in some cases the form alone must suffice. With this kind of thinking it can easily happen that the religious motivation will be overlooked if the religious formalities are present. A powerful religious apparatus compensates for a lack of justice and love. One can oppress the stranger, the widow, and the orphan and yet find edification in one's beautiful religion. "Here is the Lord's temple, here is the Lord's temple!" The mystical flame of devotion can blind one to the absence of plain moral integrity. Yes, one can have religious power and profundity and enthusiasm and still be a very ordinary person, or even an unusually vulgar, mean person — which is a puzzle that has troubled many people already.

Religious pleasure-seeking, a poisonous weed, can grow well in such soil; it is right at home there. Those in whom the weed grows cannot get enough in the way of religious exultations, enunciations, edifications, and profundities. They ransack one "religious personality" after another for whatever he or she has to offer; they run from one (Catholic or Protestant, old-fashioned or modern) place of grace to another, and in their consuming search for pleasure become ever more impoverished. They make out of religion something like a sophisticated sport and get themselves enmeshed in all kinds of absurdities. Derangement in crude sensuality is often not far off.

It is exactly the same way as when one pursues morality purely for the sake of morality, or art for the sake of art, without being fully committed to it in all that one does. Morality then becomes a sport, purely a matter of form, an ever-proliferating set of laws, a tyranny, a burden. Art then becomes pure artistry that evolves out of its inner emptiness into something of a tasteless and abnormal nature. So is it also with religion when it is pursued for its own sake. Like morality and art, it incurs the curse of the words "who seeks to save his soul will lose it."

Where the Kingdom of God is, however, there it can be said that "he who loses his life for my sake will find it." Here religion for religion's sake does not count for anything. It is the most needless, ridiculous, presumptuous, and dangerous of games. "I hate, I despise your feasts," said God through the mouth of the prophet, "and I take no delight in your solemn assemblies. Even though you offer me your burnt offerings and cereal offerings, I will not accept them.... Take away from me the noise of your songs, to the melody of your harps I will not listen. But let justice roll down like waters, and righteousness like an everflowing stream" (Amos 5:21–24).

It does no good to have religion; one must have the things of God and man. He who has those will (particularly if not hindered by religion) have a "religion" that will develop within himself. He will need God as his helper. He will come to him pleading. With heart and mind he will seek to know God. He will seek for himself times of meditation and concentration. He will, under certain circumstances, push the world away for the sake of God. He will direct all his striving toward one goal: to serve God alone and no other gods, especially not himself. But this "religion" will then be totally tied to striving after the Kingdom of God and his righteousness. It will be real in the best sense of the word. No excess, sport, or artistry will enter into it; everything will be healthy, natural, taken for granted as natural—and like nature this life will be at once both simple and rich.

The difference between this true "religion" and religion is like the difference between nature and the hothouse. Where with an air of the superiority of religion one withdraws from the ordinary and rough work of the world in order to save his soul and to find God in the "stillness" or the "assembly," where one does not desire merely to strengthen or orient oneself for new work and battle but wants merely to follow religious methods and practices, there the opposite will occur: one will fall away from the God who wants to build his Kingdom in the world, and will therefore become ensnared in the deceitful webs of his own thoughts and perhaps come to doom. There is a strong law at work here. The God who is known in the Kingdom of God lets himself be found only in the rough and ordinary work for his Kingdom.

It is here that the recovery of "religion" must start. It is inherent in men that they understand this God. Where individuals or whole communities stand for that which is a part of being human, for righteousness and justice, freedom and truth, love and purity, and where they do it in the name of God, there God is understood and honored—even by the godless. On the other hand, much of the "godlessness" in the world results from observing the practices of a religion that denies God. Amidst the "godless" who yearn and fight for a better world is the Kingdom of God; among the others is religion. We will achieve the healthy state of affairs that we need when we do not force religion on anyone and do not drill anyone in it, but when we rather seek the Kingdom of God—that is, when we have an ultimate concern, when we count every great and pure cause as somehow our own, when we can be counted on. Then we will be able to understand each other when talking about God; then his name will appear on our lips at the right time; then knowledge of him will rise like the sun.

Furthermore, religion comes to the point of seeking itself and abrogating the place of God when it tries to conceal the absence of his Kingdom. Out of this self-seeking come other consequences as well. Religion is very much concerned with preserving itself. Since it does not draw its life from the living God but rather from itself, it has to seek all kinds of means for keeping itself alive. It enters into partnership with the world. It seeks citizenship there. It depends on money, on ecclesiastical or state power, on the ruling order of society, on morality, or even on immorality. In return, it promises its benefactors spiritual support. It offers them consecration or at least toleration. Thus it becomes a conservative power—yes, the most conservative power that there is. This element of constancy lies in its very nature; it is stagnant. Conservatism of itself, of course, is not bad, just as radicalism and a revolutionary nature are not intrinsically worthy of praise. There is, however, an obstinancy that leads away from God. God is a living God; he is life itself. When something stagnates, it departs from him. When the world as such receives the consecration of religion, which then works as holy incrustation, both world and religion suffer the damages together. Thus there is created a religion that is truly the strongest reactionary power in the world today, a religion that from time immemorial has restricted truth and life and has earned the hatred of free spirits, that has throughout history and in many cultures earned the epithet "écrasez l'infâme."

Its critics are right: religion *is* the strongest reactionary power in the world today. But we want to add that the Kingdom of God is the strongest revolutionary power, the strongest driving force, the innermost disturbance of life in history. Whereas the priest was the greatest restrictor of freedom, truth, and justice, the prophet was the people's most forceful advocate.

We will go on from here one step further and express the last and most difficult thing. From the mouths of those who attack religion we hear again and again that it is the worst of all evils that burden mankind. This is what the freethinkers, the social democrats, say, and this is what many democrats who do not say it aloud think. Maybe they will once open the book of horrors committed in history and show us that its bloodiest and blackest pages were written by religion. Then we will stand embarrassed. We will try to defend the attacked. We will try to distinguish between the true and the false religion and explain that it was false religion that caused all that is being attributed to the true religion.

It might be better to drop the defense and admit that yes, religion is the most terrible power in history. Naturally, it is also the most wonderful, glorious, blessed power, but along with that it is also the most terrible one. These are two sides of the same coin. Religion is a matter of the spirit, and thus it comprises both heaven and hell. Religion belongs to the world. It is the world's most glorious blossom, but also its most terrible protuberance. Instead of overcoming the world, it adds to the world its substance, an element of eternity and absoluteness, and raises it that way to the supernatural. Thus it becomes the realm that the demons particularly like to invade. Thus man is led astray by it to do evil things that he would never do naturally. Thus originate the wildest of horrors. Thus grows a fanaticism, a force of hatred, a power of lies that could not flow from other sources. Religious fanaticism, religious hatred, and religious lies are worse than their parallel worldly forms, and they flow inexhaustibly from this source.

Above all, it is bad that religion sanctifies what otherwise would be overcome, that it covers with a luster what without question would otherwise appear to be bare and common. From time immemorial it has done so. This is especially evident today when we think of war. For a long time churches and theologians have cast the luster of religion on it. They have fought most passionately against the peace movement. They have promoted that "religious elation" which was a part of the great madness by which the world was thrown into an abyss. And today they are the greatest propagators of nationalism and militarism. Some of them are bloodthirsty villains. Only they could get the idea of putting Jesus in a trench or behind a machine gun. One can perhaps go even farther and say that it is religion that lies at the root of war. War is of a piece with religion, for war is a cosmic power. It is a part of that strange curse that lies upon humanity and in many ways holds it in a sphere of degradation, in a demonic state. Along with alcoholism, Mammonism, and sexualism it belongs to a cohesive world, and out of this world rises also religion—not all religions, but that religion which is really the worst of all evils.

Religion is the worst of all evils. But above religion is God, the true God. He is not to be confused with it. And where one comes into relationship with him, where one comes in his light, there is his Kingdom. Where the Kingdom is, there is no serfdom, but liberation. There the demons flee. There it is not the human spirit that is speaking, but the Spirit. There blusters not the religiously exalted nature, but there bids a holy will. There is no more the world, but the realm of the supernatural. There nothing exists but purity, freedom, goodness, light. There nothing separates the truly divine from the truly human. There man finds his home. There nature comes truly into its own. There everything is realized that religion in the deepest sense wants. In the dissolution it is fulfilled.

The Kingdom of God has existed alongside and above religion throughout history. At one time it battled with it; at another time it breathed into it something of its nature. In Israel it shone clear and victorious; in Jesus it became the new dawn of history. Jesus Christ destroyed religion and brought the Kingdom of God to light. Jesus Christ is the end of religion. This is the greatest fact of history. We, however, press forward through night and wasteland, in battle and chaos, marching out of the kingdom of religion to the Kingdom of God and mankind; we press forward to the world of Christ, which slowly rises above the waters of the great flood.

And now we encourage those among the "godless people" who are searching for God to look at Christ in this new light. We urge them to examine the "religious problem" from this perspective. We urge them to seek God in this way. They should seek not a religion but the Kingdom of God. This is the way forward.

Ragaz found the alliance of religion with various forms of power deplorable. He called it Pfaffentum, "clericalism." This meditation, written in 1917, appears in Weltreich, Religion und Gottesherrschaft *(vol. 1, pp. 273 –99).*

THE KINGDOM OF GOD AND CLERICALISM

IF ONE WERE TO ASK me what is the worst of the evils that plagues our world, I would know right away what I would say... clericalism.... What is clericalism? Who is a cleric? Here we have to correct a great misunderstanding. If one talks about clericalism, one thinks immediately of clergy.... However, by clericalism we do not mean simply clergy. Though there may be pastors who are clerics, and though there is a particular temptation for clergy to fall into clericalism, there are also many clergy who are not clerics, and many clerics who are not clergy. Clericalism is a general phenomenon that occurs everywhere in the field of humanity, and it is this phenomenon that we want to consider....

Are we far off the mark when we say that clericalism arises where religion, using wrong means, becomes a matter of power?

Religion as power and power as religion beget clericalism, constitute it. Its essence, you see, lies precisely in the fact that religion becomes power and power becomes religion. Thus from both "religion" and "power" emerge some refined—indeed, the most refined—forms of evil, as well as its coarse—indeed, its coarsest—forms.

The desire for power in connection with religion can come simply from the world. Religion is expected to grant power to something that is quite unreligious by using its own power for the world's purposes. The presupposition is that religion really is a power, and it is called upon to exercise that power especially in situations in which it has a great influence on the sentiments. In this regard, sometimes the state, sometimes an economic order, sometimes an isolated worldly action uses religion as a proof, as an inspiration or a halo, as a means of stimulating the greatest passion. This gives rise to the famous union of throne and altar as well as to the idea that certain social conditions that serve the interests of the ruling class amount to a God-given order. The World War has illustrated this point in a diverse variety of ways. In order to be bearable, the war had to be given a religious basis and explanation. There emerged a "religious exaltation," a religious war ideology (war theology). When the fires of war threatened to die out, religion had to fan them up again. The fact that bells were made into cannons just as cannons had often been made into bells is an eloquent symbol of this relationship....

Clericalism arises in all these situations. Everywhere religion is supposed simply to support, sanctify, or glorify aims that are basically worldly... there is clericalism.

Let us look at the bond between religion and power from the perspective of religion. Here we encounter still more refined but perhaps also more dangerous forms of the problem. If we are to see the whole problem and avoid unfairness, we must realize that there is a correct, permitted, and in fact *required* form of relationship between religion and power. Religion must wish to have power over the world, or, more accurately, it must wish that God might have power over the world: the Kingdom of God wants to be the power, the *only* power, that remains when all others are conquered; it wants to overcome all worldly powers. In general, he who says "God" says "power." We seek God in order to come out of weakness to power, and in the end to omnipotence. That is all in the order of things.

But this truth that stands on the border, so to speak, between God and man can be perverted through something that is purely human. One slides down the slope. First comes the temptation to use the power of the world in order to further religion. Can one not also extend the Kingdom of God through religious, political, or social power — that is, through priestly authority, imposing religious organizations, energetic and systematic agitation, pious halos and supernatural mysteries, state power and social prestige? May one not draw the masses who are not open to purely spiritual force to a higher life through such perceptible means? Should not money, too, be made available for it? If one can win the world for God, should one not use such means? The tempter stands before Christ. He offers to make religion available to him in the form of social help, or of magic, or of political power, if he will only decide to do a small thing in return—pay homage to him. Where the tempter triumphs, the church takes the place of the Kingdom of God and clericalism takes the place of discipleship — perhaps at first in a striking form, as in the case of Dostoievsky's Grand Inquisitor; the coarser form, however, always follows....

Every relationship of religion and power is dangerous. It is so among the pastorate because an official has to represent a particular order, an authority. To want to guard this authority and to act accordingly are very immanent temptations. Those who proclaim the Word, transmit knowledge, and deliver sermons and wedding and funeral meditations may in so doing gain approval or have success; at any rate, they want success. It is quite human, and with the flip of the hands, one becomes tied up with special interests, with a smaller or a bigger interest in power, and then one is already close to clericalism. Out of a man who wanted to serve God's Kingdom emerges a representative of a vested interest....

Thereby we come to another characteristic of clericalism that has always been conspicuous: unbelief — an unbelief incredible in the representatives of belief. In fact, there is a psychological unity of a simple sort between clericalism and unbelief. He who believes in God—really believes in him—has such a power that he needs no other. He is united with the power of God. He knows that God accomplishes whatever is necessary to realize his plan and his Kingdom; he knows that if God does not accomplish it, no human power will. This, however, doesn't make the believer lay his hands in his lap or lead him to excessive use of such pious phrases as "God alone will provide." Precisely because he believes it, he doesn't say it often. He knows that it is enough to place himself at God's disposal. He knows that God really can work alone, but he also knows that God wants to work through people, that he abhors plain unilateral action. That is the basis of the deep contradiction between genuine faith in God on the one hand and the urge for and belief in power on the other. A person who really has faith needs pure means, for he believes that only in that way will something good be accomplished. Furthermore, he is not interested primarily in achieving some religious results; rather, he seeks to advance God's Kingdom—and the Kingdom will advance only where the power of the good rules, for therein it has its being. He who has a genuine faith is also spiritually free: he is so sure of God that he can respect views about him other than his own; he can also let doubt, and particularly the doubter, do as it or he pleases without anger, without coercion because he knows that God will take care of himself. Let our concern be that we serve him well ourselves.

However, where genuine faith is lacking, a different approach and attitude becomes apparent. One feels one has to do things himself because God won't do them. One becomes angry over doubt and the doubter, and since one doesn't feel strong enough himself to battle and conquer them spiritually, one turns to external weapons, to church power, state power, or other power. The fire that is lacking from above must be replaced with a fire from below, a material or spiritual burning stake. Or one turns to some evil means of warfare—to degradation of the opponents, to sophistry, or to the arts of eloquence. All ingenious politicking, all rhetoric, simply hides a lack of faith; where God's reality grips the soul everything is simple and childlike.

Naturally, a pastor need not be a cleric. Precisely through his struggle with his office he can be freed from clericalism and thus become altogether human. This is to say that we are not speaking against pastors, but rather for them. We have to recognize the deadly enemy in order to escape from him. That the danger is extremely great none of us can honestly deny; it is dangerous to make a profession out of religion. One develops too easily a wrong intimacy with things that are holy. One becomes a specialist, and we know that to be a specialist in godly things can be disastrous; one becomes an expert, and to claim expertise in the field of piety is a terrible error....

If clericalism grows out of the relationship between religion and power, then the way to combat it becomes clear: one must break that relationship.... If the churches should rise to new life somehow, then the power that they would win would be a free, purely spiritual power.... Out of the false union of God and the world there arises clericalism; with the dissolution of that union, clericalism will disappear. If in the place of the false friendship there should at first arise enmity, then let us bless this development! When religion once stops blessing the powers that be and starts pronouncing judgment upon them, clerics will no longer be appointed....

We have rejected the identification of clerics with pastors, but we have also seen that the transformation of one to the other is easy, dangerously easy. But in conclusion, let it also be emphasized that this transformation is not automatic, that it is by no means a necessary occurrence. There are, as we said, enough pastors who are not clerics, and there are enough clerics (both male and female) who are not pastors. Still, there is nothing more important for a pastor and a professional representative of religion in general than to say to himself, "Don't become a cleric at any price! Your soul is at stake. Keep away from the temptation of power as from the worst enemy. As a representative of the cause of the Son of Man, be first of all a human, a natural, beautiful, free person—yes, be more of a human, a human to a higher degree, in a higher sense than others, and let that be your best credential...."

While warning against the danger of Bolshevism as practiced in the Soviet Union, Ragaz also warned against the "spirit of Bolshevism" evident in Western countries. This article appeared in the November 1918 issue of Neue Wege. Parts 1–3 have been abridged; parts 4 and 5 are translated in full.

THE BATTLE AGAINST BOLSHEVISM

1. What It Is All About

THE WORLD WAR is over, but now the danger of an international civil war hangs over mankind like a heavy cloud. And on that cloud is written in large letters the name "Lenin."

2. Bolshevism from Above

Precisely defined, Bolshevism refers to Lenin's dictatorship of the proletariat as practiced in Russia. In a more general sense, Bolshevism means rule over a majority by a minority. That kind of Bolshevism we have in our society, too, for we are ruled by a capitalist minority. Often people battle Bolshevism for pocketbook reasons, though they are actually practicing minority rule themselves. Our opposition is different. We fight as socialists against a perversion of socialism. It is hard to tell which international threatens us most—the red or the gold. Our banks are closely tied to rule by the moneyed minority.

3. Bolshevism from Below

Even our labor unions get caught up in the spirit of Bolshevism, for there, too, a minority often controls a majority. Leaders give out simplified analyses of the social revolution and do not tolerate different views. Our dominant social democratic papers are Leninist, often to the point of fanaticism. Even in social democratic circles we value power more than truth.

4. Bolshevism as a Danger to the World

Not only our nation, but the whole world is threatened by

Bolshevism. If worst comes to worst, then there will be not only a Swiss but also a worldwide catastrophe. The grouping of the powers in this instance is quite clear. On the one side stands the new democracy which wants to transform the world politically and socially on the basis of justice and freedom and in the light of a moral ideal. Against it stands Leninism with its proletarian imperialism. In the background, however, lurk reactionaries of every sort ready to destroy both. The battle becomes entangled in tragic ways. Democracy of the middle-class sort (best represented by Wilson) lacks socialism, and Leninism lacks democracy, so they battle each other, to the delight of the *tertius gaudens* (the third party who benefits). Everywhere there is a social democracy at work attempting to unite both truths, but, as usual, Lenin breathes his destructive, glowing fire into this effort with the unwanted result that the reactionary forces are abetted. He brings down contempt not only on all bourgeois, but also on all socialist democracies. He glorifies and practices a socialist militarism that is worse than capitalist militarism ever was. He whips all the demons into the wildest frenzy—all ostensibly for the benefit of the proletariat, but all actually serving to benefit the reactionaries.

The great danger of the hour is thus definitely Leninism—not primarily to the middle class, but to the proletariat. The social world revolution will surely come; it is only a question of *how* it will come. It should come, it must come, for our order is ripe for a revolution. But now comes the question of whether its roots will be positive or negative, whether it will arise out of yearning for a better world or out of the simple desire to overthrow the existing one, out of love or out of hate, out of the fury about hunger or out of the desire for brotherhood. If the state of the world and of Europe become such that they help Leninism to victory, then woe unto us. Then will come a tragedy the horror of which will by far supersede that of the World War. Then it will become again difficult—for many people even impossible—to hold fast to the belief that Europe and the world can be saved. Then the specter of a reaction worse than any heretofore will rise over the ruins of all ideals that had ever uplifted souls, and all of the previously toppled royal and other thrones and all the idolatrous altars will rise again. This is an hour of frightful consequences.

5. The Salvation

Whence should the help come? How do we battle Bolshevism? Bolshevism above and Bolshevism below—that is the nature of the situation. The constant change drives us to ruin.

Everywhere Bolshevism entails a belief in violence rather than justice, in dictatorship rather than democracy, in absolutism rather than freedom, in matter rather than spirit. The whole bourgeoisie professes the Bolshevist belief as much as or more than social democracy. Bolshevism is imperialism and militarism in another form. No wonder it rises out of the World War as a terrible opponent of the new world that we hope for. It is a bastard child of the old world as well as the new. It wants the socialist new world, but it wants it in the spirit of the old world. The one demand is justified; the other is not. In this mixture of right and wrong rests its magic and its curse.

But how will Bolshevism be fought? Naturally not with the weapons it is presently using—not with violence and dictatorship, not with bayonettes and machine guns, not with falsehood and deceit. Instead, it will be fought in two ways that basically are one.

First, we must eliminate the whole present order, which is basically Bolshevist in its political, social, and spiritual forms, and we must replace it with an order oriented in an opposite direction.

Second, we must do this in a new spirit, in the spirit corresponding to the new world, and with the means that are appropriate.

For the bourgeois world this involves resolutely relinquishing its attachment to the existing order and opening itself in faith to the acceptance of a new world. There is no other way. There is no other way to battle Bolshevism that would have any chance of success; there is no other hope for a return to democracy, a new Switzerland, a new Europe. Nor will halfway measures or negotiations be of any help. In practice they may be necessary, but in principle they must be given up once and for all.

For social democracy this means that socialism must assume a new orientation. While maintaining all that is great and valuable in Marxism and Leninism, it must free itself from their dogma and orthodoxy. The agitation for truth compels far more than that. For its program, socialism must find a new foundation, one that is in the deepest and soundest sense idealistic (i.e., spiritual and moral) and thereby gain new clarity, strength, and assurance of victory. Our social democracy must use its defeat for reflection and self-criticism; then the defeat will be more worthwhile than a victory. Nothing is as valuable as a well-used defeat.

For the whole world situation, however, it means that vast powers of goodwill must arise and once again give men faith in the good. They must manifest themselves in great acts of help and liberation. A peace must come that can truly be a reconciliation.

The powers of God must break the powers of hell, overthrow everywhere the kingdom of violence, and erect the kingdom of freedom. Only thus can we battle Bolshevism.

Bolshevism must be given its due, because like everything else that is strong it has some justification. Yes, we must give it its due, but differently than the way it understands itself — that is, from a higher perspective. . . .

Written in May 1919, on the occasion of President Wilson's trip to Europe, this letter by an admiring Ragaz expresses great anxiety about the emerging peace treaty with Germany and anticipates dire results if the conditions of the treaty are not substantially changed. About half of the letter appears below.

LETTER TO PRESIDENT WILSON

... WHEN YOU, most honorable Mr. President, came to Europe to introduce the Kingdom of Peace, innumerable faithful hearts followed you with high hopes but also with great fear. For you came into a world that had become almost a hell. You came into an atmosphere full of poisonous elements. You stepped upon a ground full of hidden snares and precipices. Perhaps the world has placed too high a hope in you, one lone man, and has not given you enough support.

This writer, however, saw your mission in another light. The greatest danger that threatens Europe in this hour is the prevalence of the spirit of violence that grows out of despair concerning the influence of spiritual powers. To banish this spirit by representing the ideal has been, it seems to this writer, your God-given mission. It was not necessary for you to realize your whole program, but it was necessary for the world to see you battle for the ideal and defend it to the utmost. Very much depended on that: from the human point of view, history depended on it. For one person it was almost too great a task, and therefore your most faithful followers watched your course with much anxiety.

In this hour your battle is reaching a peak. The peace treaty that had been presented to the Germans and that, one can be sure, does not correspond to your intentions, has become a great danger to the world. It was prepared at a time when the spirit of violence appeared to have already been cast to the ground and the belief in the power and strength of ideals showed signs of recovery; and now the first consequence of the treaty is a universal triumph of the spirit of violence.

As we know from reliable sources, militarism in Germany,

strengthened by the treaty, is raising up its head again. The proletarian revolution opposes it in a violent way. It is likely that this revolution will turn into a world revolution unless some saving force intervenes. If it does not, there will be a catastrophe in comparision with which the biblical flood was child's play. Hunger, despair, violence, and murder will make a real hell out of the earth, and death will reap unheard-of harvests. Nor will America be spared from it.

Against this unthinkable danger there is, humanly speaking, only one help: from Paris a light must shine that will give people back their trust in the good. The treaty with Germany must be reworked on a completely different basis, and the League of Nations must take on a form that is much more in accord with your principles. In short, the work that you have come to do must move into a new phase. Upon that depends, from a human point of view, the deliverance of the world....

This is Ragaz's clearest statement on revolutionary violence. It appeared in 1919 in brochure form and proved to be quite influential, contributing to the decision of the Swiss Social Democrats not to join the Third Internationale.

SOCIALISM AND VIOLENCE

1. Violence and the Goal of Socialism

SOCIALISM AND THE USE of force stand in basic and sharp contradiction. Socialism is based on the fundamental belief in the worth and sacredness of man, and by that I mean of each person, even the least one—indeed, of him or her above all; the very soul of socialism is a deep reverence for persons. Another way of saying it is this: socialism lives and breathes respect for the freedom of people. It takes seriously the fact that a person is an end in himself and not just a means for other purposes, that he is not just a thing, a commodity, but rather a being whose worth is unconditionally grounded in his existence, his *human* existence. In other words, socialism takes seriously the fact that a human being is something holy, in a certain sense a holy being. Because of this fundamental belief, it is the deadly enemy of every form of slavery. Because of this fundamental belief, it is against war; its antimilitarism corresponds to its innermost nature. Because of this fundamental belief, it wants to apply "thou shalt not kill" in all areas of life; it views human life as something of eternal and unconditional value. That is why socialism is a freedom movement; that is why it is a way by which humans become human. In economic life as well as in everything else, it wants to change people from commodities or slaves into people.

Would anyone among us doubt that this is the meaning of socialism? Socialism is not just an economic or political system as such; that is, it is not simply an apparatus, an external form of living. Socialism is a moral ideal, and the political or economic system is simply the means by which it gets realized, the means by which it comes to light. Without this ideal it would lose its worth. Ordinarily we do not specifically mention this, because it is so obvious. Socialism is a form of community that is based on the principle of solidarity rather than on the principle of mutual combat. This solidarity does not rest simply on egoism but on the feeling of mutual responsibility, mutual respect for the worth and sacredness of each person. Strike this factor and replace it (if you can) with pure materialism and egoism, with a mere calculation of what is useful to everybody, and you will have robbed socialism of its soul. You will have taken from it all that is great, holy, and exciting in it. This is the idealism without which all socialism collapses.

Now it seems appropriate to say that the democratic principle has the same meaning. If we speak of it, we must carefully distinguish it from the form in which it has been realized in bourgeois democracy. Even in its best form, our bourgeois democracy is just a very temporary and unsatisfactory expression of the democratic principle, since it is in general a poor representation of social freedom. The democratic principle stands high over the bourgeois democracy....

The opposite of democracy and socialism is violence. Capitalism is the exploitation of people by people, and this is possible only through force. The means of this force is money (capital) and the state power that stands behind it, climaxing in the military, but also in some spiritual powers that are put at the disposal of force, such as the press, schools, the church, religion —all of which are dependent on money and the ruling power. And let us not forget "patriotism" either. The view of man that underlies this system is that of man as simply a means to an end, a thing, a commodity, a machine, a slave. All of this belongs to the world view of materialism. The same is true of political absolutism, which divides people basically into two groups: the rulers and the ruled. Only the rulers are called to freedom and full humanity; the ruled are called to dependence and service. Within this pattern, a patriarchal form of government is to be preferred to despotic rule.

These are the two worlds that stand over against each other: the world of force and the world of freedom, the world of matter and the world of spirit. It is clear where socialism belongs.

It is also clear where Christianity belongs. May the writer yet be permitted to make this comment: There can be no doubt that Christianity is through and through democratic. If it is aristocratic, it is so only in the sense that it wants to make all people aristocrats—that is, to lift them to the highest heights—and that it believes there are individuals who can march ahead of others as leaders or pioneers. Christianity rejects all use of violence. It makes the truth that it calls for prevail by means of free proclamation, of witness through word and deed, of sacrifice and martyrdom. The Sermon on the Mount and the cross of Golgotha speak clearly enough to anyone who is not a sophist. Yes, the last word of Christianity is this: the suffering of the innocent on behalf of the guilty is the greatest driving power of history. The central battle of Western history is therefore the battle between Christ's Kingdom, which manifests itself in love and freedom, and Caesar's kingdom, which manifests itself in various forms of violence. One form of the manifestation of Christ's Kingdom is socialism. It is clear that a Christian, if he is a socialist, cannot endorse the principle of force. He can understand force, but at the very least he will refuse to recognize it as a valid principle. One cannot expect anything else from him.

But it becomes clear after this explanation that socialism and violence also oppose each other as fire and water. Socialism wants to raise people to an honorable position, but the way to people is, as has been shown before, a perpetual, often seemingly hopeless, and yet always victorious battle against violence. We cause humanity to retrogress and we sin against the Holy Spirit who works in history to the extent that we offer sacrifices on the altar of violence.

2. Violence and the Way to Socialism

... How can, how should socialism come to power? We hear the war cries of two opposing camps. One cries, "Through democracy!"; the other, "Through dictatorship of the proletariat!"

Through democracy. What does it mean? It means roughly this: the way to socialism must be in accord with its goal. It should, at least as far as humanly possible, avoid violent methods. Then there remain three points. First of all, one needs to convince as many people as possible, especially the workers, of the truth of socialism.... Second, one has to use democratic forms of politics where they are available and create them where they do not yet exist. Third, we have to educate people for socialism....

Over against this democratic method stands the so-called Bolshevist way, which uses the slogan "dictatorship of the proletariat." It sharply criticizes democracy. "You are trapped," it says, "in a democratic ideology, for you believe in a political democracy on the basis of the present political order. But can't you see that this is only a betrayal, and that what we actually have before us is a despotism, an absolutism, namely, the dictatorship of the bourgeoisie? The present state is a class state; its officials are trusted men of the bourgeoisie. The class state uses all the means at its disposal to hold down the proletariat. The sharpest and crudest form in which this power is visible is the military....

"What can the proletariat do? It must break this dictatorship. How? Through the dictatorship of the proletariat. Wherein lies this dictatorship? It lies in taking away the means that the bourgeoisie possesses for maintaining power—that is, the means of production, the state apparatus, and finally the cultural apparatus, especially the press. It is simply a case of eliminating violence through violence, but an unjust kind through a just kind. Then the new, free society will be installed and there will be a genuine democracy. Then the masses will be enlightened. Then the whole economic, social, and cultural apparatus can serve socialism...."

This is the meaning of the Bolshevist dictatorship of the proletariat. We must do our utmost to understand it as correctly as possible, and to gain the most from it. What do we say now? The dictatorship of the proletariat has subjected democracy to strong criticism, the validity of which is hard to deny; but now we have to look at it more closely. First of all, we have to see if the "dictatorship of the proletariat" is a clear concept. And to do that, we need to ask a few questions, the first of which concerns how this dictatorship will come into existence—in a democratic way or by a minority taking power by force?...

Let us assume the latter approach, and let us pose our second question. How should a minority carry out this task of taking over and maintaining the political power? As far as I can see, there is only one way: through a military coup and a military dictatorship that evolves from it. That was the Russian way. We have to face the bitter fact that a dictatorship of the proletariat will be a military dictatorship in the service of socialism—something that gives an antimilitarist (and that is, to be sure, what a true socialist is) something to think about.

And now we come to the third question: How would this come about in Switzerland?... Our only way would be to get help from some revolutionary foreign power.

Our principal question is: Is this a good way? Do we do socialism a service if we follow or recommend this way? It is this writer's conviction, based on long and thorough reflection and on no small experience, that despite all that seems to recommend it, and despite all the attractions that it has, it is in the final analysis a bad way. We must take into account the fact that a socialism that achieves victory through violence brings on two dangers, an inward and an outward one, and they are both very serious.

First there is an outward danger. It is the simple truth that through violence one can conquer an opponent outwardly but not inwardly — that, on the contrary, an outward defeat just strengthens him inwardly. He will be resentful of his conqueror and will prepare for the revolt against him. He will also be helped by a well-known fact: the victor will in time encounter difficulties.

The glory of his cause will decline. He will become tired. Many of his followers will desert him and join the former losers. Thus, the loser will have a very good prospect of throwing off the hated yoke one day....

In this whole way of thinking that expects so much from violence, there is an error to which we wish to call attention at least briefly. It lies in the overestimation of political power for the building of a new social order. It cannot be denied that political power has a certain definite significance, that it can make the change easier or harder. But it has to be realized that a truly socialistic order cannot be produced by the bearers of political power through the issuance of decrees; such an order must be developed organically through the expenditure of much time and strength, effort and spirit....

But much worse is the inner danger. One needs to realize that force is a sword that can strike back at the person using it. Whoever uses force, destroys above all himself. He poisons his soul.... After one has used violence against his enemies, one will use it against his comrades who have a different point of view....

It is a law that a good cause cannot be more fatefully harmed than by being untrue to itself....

In a socialist military dictatorship the defection from the real socialism manifests itself with particular crassness. That we do not find the idea of military dictatorship unbearable is a sign of the fact that we have already been poisoned by the spirit of violence. The emergence of socialist militarism after the destruction of capitalistic militarism is one of the saddest surprises that we have witnessed in our time....

If all of this is true, then it is apparent that it is not simply a matter of distinguishing between a socialism already realized and a socialism yet to be realized. Moreover, an old truth appears to be confirmed here once again, a truth that has the power of a natural law, namely, that a cause can be realized only by the use of the means appropriate to its nature. If someone wants to build a despotic kingdom, then let him use violence; if, however, he wants to establish a kingdom of freedom, then let him use freedom. This law can be stated also in reverse: a movement remains what it was when it was started. When one begins with violence, one never gets rid of it. An inner necessity always forces one to turn to new means of force, until one ruins himself by the use of it. When one has begun with the spirit, however, then the spirit will always stir, and it will protest against the corruption through force. Thus, it is a great error to think that socialism can first be introduced by force and then later upheld without it. Yes, one may wish it, but one can't do it. Once one has subscribed to dark powers, they don't let anyone go....

In general, one cannot emphasize enough the fact that violent methods rob socialism of what it needs the most — the joyful enthusiasm of its adherents. That is always a product of freedom....

Quite different is the democratic way. Knowing that he has a good thing, he who follows it will probably also believe that all others should follow it, too. But if he then asks himself how he can bring others to his conviction, he comes up with quite a different answer: "Truth will prevail, not through the use of force but through free persuasion of others." Therein is expressed the basic perspective of all democracy and all true socialism: respect for the inner freedom of the other person, reverence for his uniqueness, the acknowledgment that he is not just a means, but a person of intrinsic value....

To this pedagogy of freedom belongs a deep belief in the truth. Truth has its origin in freedom. All freedom originates in belief, and all denial of freedom in disbelief. True democracy also recognizes the right to err. It lets error express itself out of the conviction that this is the best way for it to refute itself. It has no trust in a truth that shies away from arguments expressed in free speech and rebuttal. And it is even less convinced that freedom can be secured through subjugation. It is essentially a principle, a world view.

Here we have arrived at a point of utmost importance. Socialism stands before two alternatives and must make a choice. Either it must view itself as an absolute and despotic power or as a democratic one, either as an authoritarian coercive force or as a power of freedom. It must make a clear-cut choice between the alternatives and then resolutely accept the consequences. The worst thing is the vacillation between the two.

One hears repeatedly the charge that socialism is a new Catholic Church. There is something true in this statement insofar as it stresses the right and necessity of a community and of solidarity as opposed to an exaggerated individualism. In this respect, the charge has much truth on its side. But when one thinks that present-day socialism is dominated by Marxism, and that Marx comes from Hegel, the greatest advocate of state absolutism, a man who declared the individual conscience to be the "radical evil," then one realizes that something of this spirit of absolutism has infused socialism as a whole. In fact, we are familiar with the socialism that is only interested in changing "the conditions" without asking how these changes relate to the thoughts and sentiments of people, a socialism that focuses solely on the outward conditions—a sort of "church" or "state" —and not on the education of socialist people. Such a socialism will easily end up in despotism and absolutism. That is its nature.

But such socialism will also experience the fate that this way brings. Its kingdom will soon fall, just as each kingdom of violence has fallen. Indeed, it will fall even sooner, because it has a built-in contradiction. If capitalism unites itself with force, it is in keeping with its nature, but if socialism does it, it is a defection from itself; it is unfaithfulness, and unfaithfulness is disintegration of the self. Socialist mortar that is mixed by force doesn't hold very well.

Therefore socialism has to unite two things: a powerful sense of community and a passionate consciousness of freedom. Together they bring about democracy, which is freedom in community and community in freedom. Socialism has to combine in itself the truth of Catholicism and the truth of Protestantism and thus help free the world from the one-sidedness of a confused individualism on the one hand and an authoritarian despotism on the other. Since for socialism the emphasis on community is a matter of course, special care must be taken not to betray freedom, but to make the community that it is building into a fortress of freedom.

That is therefore the meaning of this hour for socialism: it must decide if it wants to be a new, unprecedented form of slavery or a new, revitalizing form of freedom. According to the choice it makes, it will bring either an enormous breakthrough toward a great liberation or a colossal world tragedy. That is the ultimate meaning of the problem of socialism and force.

One can easily recognize that behind this either/or choice there are two world views. Behind the absolutist view is a belief either in nature or in some other kind of coercive power that rules the world. Behind the democratic view is the belief in the creative spirit that is freedom, that wants freedom, that creates freedom, and that is the power which, if one embraces it, brings victory.

The point is that one must choose. There is no alternative.

3. Violence and the Social Struggle

Neither the goal of socialism nor the means to achieve it allow for the principle of violence; the efforts to justify violence run the risk of being unclear or erroneous. But what is the situation as far as the social struggle is concerned? Do we believe that this issue can be omitted? If not, how is this struggle to be carried on without violence? If we do not wish to put an end to present conditions by force, how else can we eliminate them?...

This is what we must win: more trust in the truth of socialism. The reason some people try to establish socialism by force is that one often turns to force when one does not believe enough in a cause. Force is always a substitute for belief. One can measure the extent of one's belief in a cause by the readiness with which one is willing to support it by all kinds of external means. Belief, however, comes from the spirit, and the spirit comes from truth. Our way requires that we strengthen ourselves anew in socialist truth, that we gain an ever-better, ever-deeper grasp of it, that we discover ever-deeper sources of it. Then the spirit will flame up with such brightness that we will attract people to socialism without force; indeed, we will be ashamed to use violence.

This is no utopia; it's just the opposite: it is the truth that we fail to recognize when we blind our vision by dogma that denies the strongest realities. I believe that the only obstacle standing in the way of socialism is socialism.

But out of the mouths of those who agree with us thus far we hear the impatient question: "How so? Should we put up with everything and anything? Are we expected to wait patiently until it pleases our opponents to give us what belongs to us? Will we not have to wait a long time? Is it not a fact that the labor movement never accomplished anything by an appeal to the sense of justice or to the Christianity of its opponents, but that all its victories were won only through a show of strength? Just where in our society does one find the power of love and justice on which one could depend? Should only we proletarians be Christians so that the others can keep exploiting us to their hearts' content? Should we alone turn the left cheek if someone has hit us on the right? Should we turn from Marx to Tolstoi?"

It is one of the most difficult human problems that we face. We will attempt to provide at least as much clarity in addressing it as we can.

Above all, we have to put aside a number of misunderstandings. In the first place, let us emphasize once again that we do not wish to evade the social struggle. On the contrary, we want to sharpen it, if possible, though in our own way. By the way, Christianity doesn't teach that we ought to endure injustice rather than struggle against it. On the contrary, it calls for a battle against injustice that goes to the point of self-sacrifice, a battle of ultimate, unconditional passion. Jesus is a fighter whose relentlessness has not been equalled. But Tolstoi, too, is one of his great disciples. The words about turning the other cheek and the like are not a call to simple passivity, but on the contrary a command to engage in a fierce battle and to bring this battle to a successful end. They mean that one must not get lured by the enemy into fighting on the same level as he does, that one mustn't try to overcome wrong with wrong, meanness with meanness, an act of violence with an act of violence, but rather that one must fight wrong with right, meanness with nobility, acts of violence with kindness and, in short, evil with good.

Now, it is surely true that Christianity has a last word that goes above all political and social struggles: the innocent suffering for a cause, persecution for righteousness' sake. That, from the Christian point of view, is the way of conquering the world. At the end of this path stands the cross of Christ. Do we want to point out this path to socialism? We answer: Yes and No.

First, No! We must distinguish between what we call politics and what we call religion (in the highest sense). Politics cannot exist without a struggle for worldly power, but religion (at any rate that religion which is in the spirit of Christ) wishes the opposite: to reject all power for the sake of God and humanity. Politics wants to rule; religion wants to serve. In this sense, socialism, as it is generally understood, is a political movement. I believe we have to say more precisely that it is a partly political, partly religious movement. It wants to break away from the old power politics, the politics of exploitation and domination of one class by another, and substitute a politics of justice, solidarity, and mutual helpfulness. Thus does socialism stand, as it were, between politics and religion. But under no circumstances can one expect of it that highest level that the Kingdom of Christ expects of its citizens. For this, certain presuppositions are essential that are not necessarily found in socialism. The wish of each Christian remains that socialism would some day dissolve in the Kingdom of God, allowing politics and religion to converge, but today we are only on the way.

Thus, we are not assuming that we should expect socialism to adopt precisely the same tactical means one finds in the Kingdom of God. It should function as a political force as much as possible, but it should be careful to follow the principles of democracy and not those of absolutism, to follow a path leading to the heights and not into the abyss.

Thus the social struggle is by no means ruled out. By "social struggle" we mean not only the struggle of ideas but also of actions. And we will not hesitate to add that we are thereby thinking also of the right to strike. We are not at all ready to admit that the strike must of necessity be a violent act. A strike is stoppage of work, a refusal to work. Shouldn't a human being have a right to strike? Isn't this one of the original human rights? Work is the only property that a worker has; he should at least be allowed to make decisions about it. But thereby is he given an enormous weapon in his hand, for society lives mostly from his work; it cannot exist without it for a day. If the worker agrees and understands, he can, on the basis of these realities, change the whole social order. He only needs to refuse to work — in individual strikes, in industrial strikes, in rural strikes, perhaps in world strikes — and he can realize everything he wants.

But then we hear from the socialist side: "How so? Isn't this violence?" And from the middle-class side resounds the question in a thousand voices: "How is it that you speak against violence and then urge people to strike?"

I answer quite calmly that refusal to work in itself is not violence, at least not in the worst sense of the word. It is not assault, it is not exploitation. It can instead be the opposite: protest against a regime of violence, a system of exploitation. Just as no one could in all seriousness accuse the conscientious objector who refuses to give allegiance to a brutal order of engaging in violence, so nobody should charge with violence the worker who refuses to work for a similar system in the realm of industry. Actually a strike against war and a strike against industry are just as related as militarism and capitalism are on the other side.

Of course I am deliberately saying that a strike does not *of necessity* entail violence, although I certainly will admit that a strike *can* be used for assault and exploitation: even a perfectly legitimate weapon can be misused....

Next comes the question of a relation between violence and written law. We shall leave undecided the question of whether a strike of government employees is illegal or not, though even if we decided that it was illegal, that would not automatically settle the whole question. Refusing to obey a written law is still not the equivalent of using violence—otherwise the command to obey God rather than man would imply a command to use violence; otherwise those early Christians who refused to offer the legally prescribed sacrifice to the emperor and those Protestants who refused to participate in the officially ordered mass would be men of violence. It is really more a question of moral right than of legal right. And there can arise a situation in which to be true to the first one must refuse obedience to the second.

That one is allowed to do what one is supposed to do is the

big gate that leads out of the rule of absolutism in all areas, in the state as well as in the church, into the land of freedom. For here emerges the right of the individual conscience, and this is the basis of democracy. Where this is not recognized, there rules force.

To disobey a written law is, of course, revolution, at least in principle. And now the original question changes into the question of the relationship between revolution and violence. What is revolution? One can understand this word in a broader and a narrower sense. In the broader sense it means simply an upheaval, a violent change, a rapid and complete replacement of one set of conditions with another. In this sense, things present no problem to us. In the narrower sense revolution means the replacement of one system with another by illegal means. Is this violence or not? One might not call it violence, and yet it might legally be considered violence. The problem, however, is not solved thereby. It can easily happen that in its meaning and by its nature the legal system can itself be illegal. An utter despotism that has all power in its hands (above all the military power, but perhaps also financial power and the power of the press) can have the appearance of legitimacy, but under this appearance it can actually mock and assault the true justice and thus damage the administration of and respect for justice for a long time. Then it is entirely in order to replace the power that is clothed with the appearance of justice with the right that has the appearance of force. One is then simply replacing fraud with truth.

We dare not let ourselves be led astray by outward appearances; we must look at the substance. One must not make a strict doctrine out of the opposition to force simply to prove the significance of the issue. Here, too, one must act out of spirit rather than in the service of the letter of some commandment; one must pay attention to the motive, not just to the actual deed, and do so with deep earnestness rather than in sophistic deception.

In this sense a social revolution without violence is also possible. We have cited the voluntary refusal to work as the prime method. We emphasize the word *voluntary*: that must remain the ideal. Workers must be challenged to work for the new order voluntarily so that no violence is introduced. This aim will be realized to the degree that socialism recovers its original spiritual power.

To be sure, the social revolution can be realized by many other means as well. Even in the present society the proletariat can exercise an enormous power, one quite different from that of the present cooperative system, which is not even socialistic. We could build upon our labor unions in such a way that they would become pillars and hotbeds of a new work culture and could give greater content to our political organizations. We could begin developing a socialist life-style that would perhaps be even more revolutionary than the economic revolution. We could smash militarism and thereby knock out the strongest pillars of the ruling system. We could work out a socialist world view that would give our cause a stronger basis and a greater clarity. And what is there that could not be done in the reformation of the press and educational programs!

In short, a very great revolution awaits us here, one that we can begin right away and without violence if we have the right spirit and the power. Why do we pursue it so sluggishly? Maybe because we put too much trust in a revolution by force, which would be easier than the revolution of the spirit—or at least we believe it would.

Thus, we can conceive of socialist change without violence —at least without violence in the evil and accursed sense of the word — and yet skepticism remains high concerning its likelihood. Even if someone agrees with this new line of thought, he will still not believe in the practicability of change without violence. He will ask, "What happens if we are determined to avoid violence as far as humanly possible, but the others are not? Can we expect that the bourgeois world will give up its domination without using every means at its disposal in the final battle? It arms itself feverishly, and its provocations are so brazen that it would be asking the impossible of the workers to expect them to continue to put up with it for a long time to come. Furthermore, the economic conditions are becoming more critical every day so that an explosion is unavoidable."

How do we answer? We answer, first of all, by a great admission that will put everything said thus far into proper perspective. We understand nothing better than that people are tempted to turn to violence. That is natural; it is in accord with human nature. It is very natural to respond to a blow with a blow, to a curse with a curse. It is very natural to want to remove by force conditions that seem unbearable. That is all part of our nature. Thus we can understand very well if in the social struggle the socialist side also turns to violence. We could understand it if all the injustice that the proletariat had endured in the course of its sorrowful history flamed up in a wild fit of anger and broke out against the existing order. One could not then say that an injustice had been done to them; they had deserved it threefold.

But the problem is this—would such violence be of service

to us? Even understandable anger can lead to great tragedies. It is likely that the flame of passion would consume us before anyone else. Precisely *our* cause would suffer, because such an action would be contrary to its nature. A noble cause is damaged more by error than is a base cause. Therefore our advice can only be to make the impossible possible. If others use force, we do not want to use it. We do not want to imitate the others; we would rather be true to ourselves.

This is once again a great old truth, a spiritual, natural law. One is most likely to succumb to an enemy if one lets oneself be lured into fighting on his ground; one is most likely to defeat him if one meets him with the weapons that fit one's own cause. So let the bourgeoisie come with all their reactionary measures; let them simply go ahead. They will hurt only themselves and provide us with propaganda. And if they come with bayonets and machine guns, then let them come. What harm can they do to us with their weapons? They can't drive us away from socialism. They can't force us to work. They can only dig an early grave for themselves.

"But won't violence break out despite everything? Won't we ourselves have to turn to violence some day?" I will again respond with an admission: it *can* happen. Let us assume that a certain measure of violence is unavoidable. Then it is our task to keep this measure as small as possible. Then we must know what a heavy responsibility we are taking upon ourselves if we turn to violence, no matter how justified. We have to know what it means to wield a two-edged sword, how all the demons awake as soon as it is pulled out of the sheath. We must know how questionable even a nonviolent revolution is, how it unleashes all sorts of evil instincts and attracts all the phantoms of hell. When in a great emergency we decide that we must turn to violence and revolution, then we should do it with fear and trembling and summon first all the good spirits. Otherwise the drawn sword will turn against us, and we will be swallowed up in the released torrent.

One thing is true in any case: whether we believe that we can succeed without violence or not, certainly every glorification of violence is a wickedness and a defection from socialism. If violence can bring us a step forward, it can also take us half a step (if not two steps) backward. Every use of violence is above all a defeat for socialism.... The ideal remains a victory without violence through the spirit and through truth.

On this basis one may answer the question of whether socialism should simply use the tactics of the Sermon on the Mount and of the cross with both a No and a Yes—that is, with a qualified No and a qualified Yes. Socialism should be buttressed as much as possible by the purest of powers so that it can be freed from the evil spirits that threaten to destroy it. It should learn to recognize those high truths by which all mankind is ultimately ruled.... It should also know that its greatest power for victory lies in that truth that is most powerfully embodied in the cross—in the love that gives of itself freely, in the sacrifice of the pure for the impure, in the suffering of the righteous for the unrighteous.

4. Bolshevism and the New Social Democracy

In conclusion, we must say something about the movement that really brought about this discourse, so-called Bolshevism. Because of it the whole question of the relationship of socialism to violence has become such a burning issue. We have already subjected to criticism some of its slogans; now we need to take a position on the whole phenomenon.

Bolshevism is a mixture of two elements: the spirit of unconditionality and the spirit of violence. From this mixture stem its virtues and its faults, its appealing power and its danger. It uses the tactics of violence much more readily than the hitherto existing social democracy. It intensifies the demand for a dictatorship of the proletariat far above the place given to it in social democracy. It depends on the capitalistic means of power (viz., the military) in a way never dreamed of before. It rejects more or less categorically the democratic principle and finds little value in the freedom of the individual: these it views as *petit bourgeois* ideals. It is thoroughly filled with dogmatism and fanaticism that leave little place for spiritual freedom. For the building of a socialist society it relies fervently on political power. Violent revolution is its messiah. Thus, Bolshevism is the fruit of an era that has incarnated its "will to power" through etatism, militarism, and capitalism, as well as through Darwinism and Nietzscheism....

But this element of violence is combined with another, which greatly strengthens the effect of Bolshevism, and that is its unconditionality. It wants the whole of socialism. It knows no compromise. It roams the whole world, or so at least it appears. It seems to offer something whole and permanent, something that goes beyond half-way measures into a new world....

What position do we take? Our position is this: we separate the two elements that make Bolshevism, and reject one part and accept the other. We reject the element of violence and accept the element of unconditionality.

We reject the element of violence. This is self-evident from what we have said before. We consider the watchword of the "dictatorship of the proletariat" to be deceitful. We detest the militarism, the dogmatic fanaticism, and the lack of freedom and breadth implicit in Bolshevism.

But we accept the unconditionality. It is justified as a criticism of the methods used up to now by parliamentary democracy. These "democratic methods" that Bolshevism refers to have worked themselves out. We think of parliamentarianism of all sorts....

It is the right of Bolshevism to try another way. In doing so, it brings honor to the truth of the movements that social democracy has treated with an undeserved low esteem. Its right is, as I see it, an immediate socialism and an immediate democracy....

This address was delivered at a Fellowship of Reconciliation meeting in Nyberg, Denmark, and was reprinted in January 1924 in Die Eiche, a German journal for social concerns.

The piece provides a sharp critique of the church. In it Ragaz suggests that Christians are by definition revolutionaries, and that Christian revolution is by nature yet more radical than political revolution, such as the French and Russian varieties. He notes, however, that those who profess to be Christians in fact tend to be the most reactionary of people, that non-Christians on the whole show far more revolutionary spirit. This, he argues, must change: Christians must come to grips with the revolutionary nature of the faith they profess. They must grapple with the issue of property and learn to live more like St. Francis. They must realistically face the issue of the "demons of violence," since reliance on violence stems from a lack of faith. He also contends that the class struggle can be overcome through reconciliation —if the reconciliation is based on truth.

The following excerpt from the speech presents his focus on the church and its responsibility to find its way to genuine Christianity.

THE CHRISTIAN REVOLUTION

IF WE WANT TO CARRY OUT the Revolution of Christ we need a new way of representing the cause of Christ. But here we are confronted with the great and weighty problem of the church. Can the church represent Christ? Is the church not religion in an official, recognized, and therefore ineffective form? Can Christ be official? Can Christ be a component of the existing world order? Is the church not simply making a bow before God on behalf of the world, which then goes on in its usual way? Is the church not thereby a hindrance to God? It would not be right if in the land of Kierkegaard we didn't pose the question of whether the Christian ecclesiastical form does not produce a fatal delusion through the pretense that the Christianity of the New Testament is at hand when in fact it is not.

Let me make a personal confession and tell you, dear friends, that this has been the greatest problem of my life. I have solved it after great inner battles by giving up my position as a professor of theology and a teacher of pastors in order to represent Christ in poverty — without assured income, but in a free and totally unofficial way. Now I am in the middle of a wilderness, of what appears to be a godless world. In my fierce battle for the Kingdom of God in the midst of this world I find that I receive no help — none whatsoever — from the church, from organized religion.

The church seems to me to be something nonessential. This is the word that keeps coming into my mind. There is much edification, consolation, and activity there, but there is no strength for changing the world; rather, the church seems to be bent on comforting the world. The church must make its representation of Christ a reality. Christ must be brought into the midst of the world. Where one expects it least, there he must be proclaimed. He must be proclaimed in the council chambers, in the workshop, in the school, on the street, in the field. That means he must come dressed in lay attire. He must be represented not by official or semiofficial civil servants but by simple folk and children of God. On the way to work and in the workshop, the worker must tell his fellow workers about Christ, and in the public gatherings he must appear.

The task must not be left to a group of religious professionals. The seriousness of the task must become real to each and every person and thus be a matter of public concern, making the priesthood of all believers a reality. Only then can the cause of Christ once more gain such power that through a new reformation it can bring about the possibility of really turning the world upside down. The Kingdom-of-God model of the cause of Christ must replace the church model. This model manifests itself in the world. It is thus that Christ enters the world and gains human stature in realities, not just in symbols. It is thus that the world becomes the sacrament by which the Word becomes flesh. A Christ restricted to the church turns into a Christ embracing the world.

*In 1924, upon the deaths of Wilson and Lenin,
Ragaz wrote an article for the Neue Wege noting
that the two men symbolized two social systems
in conflict with each other. He concluded that the
world needed to learn from both – democracy
from Wilson and socialism from Lenin. Following
are excerpts presenting the salient points of the
article.*

WILSON AND LENIN

HISTORY PERMITS ITSELF from time to time a magnificent symbolism. Such is the case with the almost simultaneous deaths of Wilson and Lenin, these two great antagonists on the socio-political battlefield of our time....

Wilson and Lenin represent above all two principles. What does Wilson represent?... I have always loved him as the man who dared to apply moral truth to politics in a new and decisive way.... At its deepest level this moral idealism was a faith, a faith in the holy God, whose will all flesh should obey. Since biblical times this faith has not been represented by anyone more forcefully than by Calvin, and Wilson of course was a spiritual descendant of Calvin. His spirit was that of American Puritanism; his democracy presupposed theocracy. Thus it was again our concern that this man represented. The spirit that essentially made our Switzerland what it is and upheld it inwardly came in him again to us, protecting and renewing us. How should we not have joyfully greeted him?

... What does Lenin represent? Perhaps in order to discuss this opposite of Wilson we should start with the difference in their cultural backgrounds. While Wilson came out of the Anglo-Saxon culture, marked by the spirit of Calvin, and representing the best in America, Lenin came out of the Slavic world, representing the Russian spirit, though in only one form (and that not necessarily the best). The Slavic soul is basically different from the Anglo-Saxon soul. Whereas the latter sees the absolute in the worth of the individual, the former sees it in the community — it wants to lose itself in the whole. Whereas the natural expression of the best in the Anglo-Saxon world is democracy, for Russians and for Slavs in general it is socialism — indeed, Communism....

...We see how intensely both of these tendencies are at work in our time. On the one hand, democracy advances. The nations, the races, the sexes, and the various age groups (I am thinking of the youth movement) demand their right to self-determination. They want to lead their own life; they demand their rights. The various minority groups want to prove themselves over against the larger societal structures. All of that is implicit in Wilson. On the other hand, there is the urge to find community, to find the greatest possible uniform patterns. The human spirit longs passionately for the absolute in order to dissolve in it. The conquests of Catholicism are in part explained by this fact. Here there is little stress on the individual; one wants the universal. One is tired of the subjective and seeks the objective. One has had enough of autonomy and wants authority. One does not care to hear any more about freedom; one yearns for some kind of dictatorship. Here there is little esteem for ethical considerations but more openness to some kind of mysticism of violence.

These contrasts between East and West reflect universal psychological contrasts. All our souls are torn by the battle between self-assertion and self-denial, between stubborn persistence in individualism and a willingness to surrender. It is thus fairly clear that both principles have a ring of truth to them, that both have a claim to being justified. What is interesting in considering the contradiction between these two powers is that life itself seems to comprise an eternal polarity as it advances through the tension between them. Neither one of these principles alone will suffice to shape the new sociopolitical world. We need, in this fundamental sense, both Wilson and Lenin. Democracy cannot be realized today without socialism; but neither can socialism be realized without democracy. Mere self-determination will tear the world asunder and lead ultimately to a new war, just as mere socialism (in the sense of absorption of the individual into the society) will lead to a new tyranny....

Both principles must work together in building the new world — both Wilson and Lenin — which means, as has been said, neither Wilson alone nor Lenin alone. The two conflicting principles must be reconciled; they must be understood as the two sides of one single truth. Then they will be liberated from their errors....

Ragaz experienced many ups and downs in his social struggles. There were times when all the humanizing forces seemed to be in full retreat before the powers of the kingdom of evil. In such times of discouragement he relied on biblical resources for assurance of God's ultimate victory. The following sermon from Isaiah manifests a biblical hope expressed during a time of despair. Delivered in 1929, it appeared in print in Das Reich und die Nachfolge.

A REMNANT WILL REMAIN

"...like a terebinth or an oak, whose stump remains standing when it is felled. The holy seed is its stump."

— Isaiah 6:13

THERE IS A COMFORTING THOUGHT that appears in the writings of the prophets again and again: "A remnant will remain." Should everything that one has set one's hopes on go to ruin, should everything that was high and abundant fall under the lightning of God's judgment, yet so long as there is something in it that has come from God, something in which the hope, faith, and suffering of the faithful has been invested, something that has been moistened with the heart's blood, it will prove to be the holy seed out of which new life will come.

This thought — and it is more than a mere thought — is expressed impressively and forcefully in the powerful report of the calling of Isaiah. He is called. With hesitation and fear born of his inadequacy and unworthiness for this commission, he nevertheless obeys in the end. "Here am I, send me." But what is he supposed to proclaim? Something very unusual, quite contradictory: "Hear and hear, but do not understand; see and see, but do not perceive. Make the heart of this people fat, and their ears heavy, and shut their eyes; lest they see with their eyes, and hear with their ears, and understand with their hearts, and turn and be healed." This means: "When you proclaim the word of God you must not expect that people will understand his will and obey it; rather you must be prepared for complete nonacceptance and complete failure. Your object lessons about events will not be understood, your words will fade into thin air, your preaching for repentance will only harden people's hearts, and your promises will be ridiculed. And it will keep getting worse." Truly a gloomy outlook, a peculiar stimulus for prophetic work. It is as if later experiences were mingling with the recollections of the calling and as if an element originally existing in embryonic form were assigned a greater role. Isaiah responded to God by asking "How long, O Lord?" and he received the following answer: "Until cities lie waste without inhabitants, and houses without men, and the land is utterly desolate, and the Lord removes men far away, and the forsaken places are many in the midst of the land. And though a tenth remain in it, it will be burned again, like a terebinth or an oak, whose stump remains standing when it is felled. The holy seed is its stump."

Then it happened that way. Judah's oak fell, just as Israel's terebinth had fallen earlier. The people wandered in exile—first one group, then the other. The temple in Jerusalem became a ruin and the holy city a home for jackals. Everything seemed to be over and done. But there was a remnant. There remained what the prophets had believed in, fought for, suffered for, foretold. There had been very few who had accepted the message, and what did they amount to, these uninfluential people against the multitude of politicians, priests, false prophets, and the blind masses of people? These few, lowly and scorned, however, these so-called traitors to their country, they were the holy seed out of which Israel rose once again. Much more: the prophetic word and work were the holy seed out of which the tree grew, the seed that became the life of humanity. Ultimately out of Israel came Christ, and his kingdom—the Kingdom of God—will be the last word of history.

I was thinking recently about this watchword "A remnant will remain" when I was reflecting on the Swiss situation. It seems to me to be the last, the one and only comfort for our situation, since everything else looks dismal. All things that have been tried for the sake of renewal and preservation of Switzerland in these decisive times, whether by individuals or groups, all the new goals that have been presented, all the new life-styles that have been tried, all the faith, hope, and love that have been advocated, all the justice and grace that have been proclaimed— let's admit it openly: little or nothing has come of any of them. Politicians, priests, and intellectuals have closed their ears and hardened their hearts, and the masses, following their wild and stupid instincts, have allowed themselves to be moved by the slogans of the demagogues as if they had never heard a thing about the word of God concerning judgment and salvation. The leaves and blossoms have fallen from the tree of our hopes, and who knows but that one day a catastrophic lightning will strike the trunk also. Our people have abundantly — superabundantly — earned this day of judgment.

So, what now then? Shall we take our hand from the plow? Shall we give up? No, for a remnant will remain. Of that we may be sure. Blossoms and leaves may wither; many, very many of our efforts may appear to be peripheral and temporary. Indeed, the trunk may be destroyed. The historical catastrophe may wipe out our land, a catastrophe that the politicians, journalists, priests and false prophets, business magnates, men of letters, intellectuals, as well as the deluded masses will "draw with cords" (this, too, is a prophetic picture! [see Isa. 5:18]). Nevertheless, the holy trunk will remain. What our hearts have fertilized with their blood will remain. The tree will grow up again in due time, more beautiful, more glorious than we had hoped. Switzerland will prevail because of what a small circle of people from various backgrounds and parties, scattered throughout the land, have believed, hoped, loved, and suffered on her behalf. This is the power of resurrection through which she will arise from the catastrophe. Therefore, let us continue to work in confidence in the midst of all disappointments, all failures, all misery; let us work ever more faithfully, ever more genuinely, ever more determinedly, cleansed again and again by the fire of God's judgment. Nothing, absolutely nothing will be done in vain. A remnant will remain, and in this remnant will be preserved everything that we have done with God's help — yes, everything that we have done merely out of our weak hearts and with our dull minds, so long as we have done it in faithfulness. It may be diminished in size, but it will be purified, blessed, sanctified.

We must view, I think, all of our actions in today's world from the same perspective. We do not deny at all that, along with the expectation of coming judgments and catastrophes that we have fostered throughout our lives, we have also cherished within us noble hopes and have seen before us shining goals for our work and our struggles. The war has enhanced a sense of both judgment and hope (theologians call it the eschatological-apocalyptic expectation). This hope was — and is — not only the highest, the ultimate of all hopes, the Kingdom of God itself, but also a human, temporary hope expressed in the realization of things such as democracy, socialism, triumph over war, a new spiritual culture, better societal forms, and many other things of this nature. However, if we do not wish to deceive ourselves, we had better admit that the present world shows little promise of their fulfillment. Neither democracy nor socialism flourish in the world of today: nor does any new culture for that matter. What we are confronted with is mostly decay.

This period may last for a long time—perhaps longer than the present young generation. We shall witness mostly the continual devastation of spiritual life, the progressive deterioration of culture, a gradual mechanization, brutalization, and demonization. It will become ever more futile to speak about culture. Day by day we will sink deeper into barbarism of every sort. Democracy? Socialism? A new culture? One can only laugh. The dictatorship of money and power, bread and circuses, the wildest outburst of the most godless selfishness and brutality—that is the outlook for the near future. Indeed, the outlook can become even darker.

Does this whole present world have any kind of future at all? Is not at least the decline of the West sealed? Do not all the signs point in that direction for those who can see? Is the world given any time of grace? Are we coming to the great turning point described in the account of the Second Coming of Christ? Will we not experience in increasing measure the emergence and the rise of all godless, demonic, even Satanic powers? Will not the anti-Christ manifest more and more clearly his sovereignty? Or let's consider the other side of the coin: Should we not concentrate all our strength and our yearning on the one goal, the coming of God and his Kingdom, which brings not only judgment but above all grace? Why should we still occupy ourselves with various temporal human matters at such a time, in view of such signs? After all, it is all in vain.

How shall we respond to this?

Let us say it again: No matter what turn current developments take, a remnant will remain. What we do today for these noble human goals and hopes, for democracy, socialism, and peace, a new culture may look like something that has been scattered in sand and swamp. For the time being it may seem that it has no future; nevertheless, it will not be in vain. It is a contribution to the kingdom of good that will outlast all time. That is the meaning and purpose of all history. It is the holy seed of a future that may be near or distant. It does not really matter which. In regard to what we do today, I would say that if it is something necessary, something pertinent, and not just something made up or dreamed up, then it is needed also for the future: it prepares the future, protects its roots. And it will also continue to exist when something new grows up out of the holy stump. In history there is never a total break-off or a cessation; there is always a linkage and continuity. What the prophets of Israel did in apparent hopelessness when the state was conquered and ceased to exist determined the future. A second Isaiah built upon Isaiah, and a psalmist built upon Jeremiah, until out of the almost dried-up root of Jesse the shoot sprang forth, a shoot that became the salvation of the world. At the time when the ancient world with all its glory was going to its grave, in the midst of the noise of the Vandals who stormed his African episcopal city, Augustine wrote his *City of God*, a work that could have been written perhaps only at such a time, and it proved to be a work that pointed beyond the fall of that civilization to a new era.

Let us therefore labor on with confidence. Let us work for democracy, socialism, world peace, new education. If we do it not as a sport but as a commission, in organic connection with the developments that God willed for our time, then we will work in the best possible way for the future, for all times. And if all immediate aims of our work should become worthless, should be superseded, then our will to work might still retain its worth, our service to God and man might retain its worth. They would be preserved, would become the holy seed.

One could argue, of course, that work in which one would see no immediate results, a work with goals that were so long-range, could not sustain the joy necessary for a successful completion. It would lead to resignation. This thinking is certainly not entirely without merit. In many respects, resignation is our human lot. And resignation can paralyze. But it can also strengthen and enliven. By freeing people from illusions it can awaken hope; by blocking false paths it can lead to that deep source of all action which springs from the Eternal. And everything that stems from the Eternal lives and registers an immediate success. Who can grasp this, let him grasp it. But let me add that beyond the decadence of our time a new world is arising; the dawn of a new day shimmers over the mountaintops, and a ray of a new sun falls here and there into the valley. The greatest hopes of all are bound to the picture of such a time in the world's history, a time in which there is the hope for peace, the prospect for a unification of peoples, and yes, even the prospect of a new divine era. Shouldn't that be a deep and powerful source of enthusiasm? And if certain goals should really be outmoded in the present form, could they not arise again in a new form? Instead of democracy, could there not emerge a new form of brotherhood that would also safeguard freedom? And instead of a new culture that knows no God, could there not emerge a new life with God? Couldn't the goals that we serve today be disguised figures that, when they remove their masks, are more glorious than we thought? Could not the great need of our time—I think especially of the spiritual need—be a first stage and a prerequisite for a complete change, a turning to

God and to men? And could it not be that sometimes through our perseverance toward outmoded goals, we actually manage to press forward toward goals that are in fact valid, whereas without this work we might suffocate in sand and swamp?

To summarize we might say that if God lives and we work for him, "doing deeds" with him, then we can work with joy even in a time such as ours, for God is joy in all times; he is, in fact, the only joy. In all times he has work for us that entails joy in him. Whoever serves him will not work without hope, nor without "success."

This is valid, if we may say so, even for the most extreme case. Even if the end of time were near, we would have to work, and we wouldn't work in vain. We must be found working when the Lord comes. Only he who works remains awake; those who don't work fall asleep, as the foolish maidens fell asleep, and start dreaming. But we can work only on human, concrete, temporary projects. In these God meets us. It is not beneath him to do this—only theologians and superpious people think so, but the Bible teaches the opposite; it is, so to speak, a sign of his humanity that he meets us in such a way. If we do the work that we find to be necessary, if we fight for human, noble, high goals even though they be temporary, then we are preparing the Second Coming of Christ, then we are preparing *ourselves* for it. Yes, we can and must dare to say that it is not in the empty rooms of theology and piety but in the struggles with the God-given tasks of our time that we feel the breath that suggests the coming of God and our hearts are filled with the highest joy that is God himself. And we may also be certain that God needs us, for he cannot come to the inactive, to the sleeping; he can only come to the prepared, the eager, the waiting—and these are the working ones. Therefore, it is precisely in these times that our work is more necessary, and therefore, I repeat, also more joyful than before, if only we understand everything correctly.

Finally, we can relate this hopeful viewpoint to our own personal lives. It is true here also. Much, much (perhaps most) of what we individuals strive for fades away. Flowers and leaves wither and drop. What we longed for does not happen. There are catastrophes and failures great and small. They are uniquely tragic in the lives of the people we call great. Little was realized immediately of the hopes of Luther, Zwingli, Pestalozzi, or Wilson (dare I also mention him?); so much went in the other direction. Zwingli fell at Kappel, struck down by a mercenary. A year after Luther's death, Karl V and Duke Alba stood at his grave. As a forsaken old man, Pestalozzi reflected in Neuhof upon the failure of his work. Wilson died not knowing what would happen to his work.

But here also we see that a remnant will remain. Out of the stump of the tree knocked down by lightning grew up the Zwinglian and Lutheran Reformation, and perhaps we will live to see the day when the last and the best that they wished for will blossom anew. Out of old Pestalozzi's swan song has come a mighty chorus of new love for the people, and it is getting stronger. Wilson's League of Nations lives. And so it will be also with the small ones—even the smallest. No matter how much of our work may vanish, no matter how many flowers and leaves may fall—indeed, no matter how many branches may break off— and no matter how many catastrophes and failures may point to the end, a remnant will remain. Out of the innermost kernel of what we have believed and hoped for, out of its holy, God-planted roots, it will grow up, in a different form perhaps from the one we had anticipated, but nevertheless looking unexpectedly beautiful and glorious. Out of the worst defeats and the greatest disappointments, out of the most bitter heartaches it will grow up. The greatest preliminary failure is perhaps a prerequisite for the final success. Let us remain confident and let us be ever more faithful, more thorough, more determined, more pure, and above all let us sow willingly the holy seed of suffering, so that someday, when we no longer see it with our earthly eyes, it will stand tall and strong in God's field. It is perhaps good that we do not see it now.

Once more let me say it in the strongest and holiest sense, "a remnant will remain."

This is the first of four lectures that were later printed in the book Von Christus zu Marx, von Marx zu Christus. *Appearing in 1929, this volume was translated into several languages and is probably Ragaz's best-known work outside of Switzerland. The lecture begins with a parable about a marriage, through which Ragaz tries to clarify the relationships among Christianity, socialism, and communism.*

WHICH WORLD VIEW BELONGS TO SOCIALISM?

ONCE UPON A TIME there was a youth in whom the flame of turbulent idealism burned. He was driven to rebellion not only against the obvious evils that he saw around him but also against much that was generally accepted as true, good, and holy in his family and in his general environment, all of which struck him as low and untruthful. He felt that he had found a superior truth that wanted to revolutionize everything in existence. This youth met a noble and beautiful young maiden who won his whole passionate heart. But their mutual love ended soon in a tragic way. For the young lady, as beautiful in body and as noble in disposition as she appeared to be, was unable to understand the impetuous youth. She was too strongly attached to her family and her environment. To her these seemed to be the incarnation of all that was good and worthy. She loved the youth sincerely, but precisely because of that she felt fully committed to draw him away from his destructive errors (for thus his thoughts appeared to her) and to win him over to her side. To be sure, she had moments when the intensity of his beliefs and desires gripped her also, and she was always ready to admit the validity of his views on this or that point, but still she couldn't break loose from her old world; in fact, in the end there developed in her soul something like a hatred against everything in the soul of the beloved that contradicted the ideals that she would have liked to implant there.

Thus a sharp conflict developed quickly between the strong love that these two noble people had for each other and the loyalties that they had to serve and from which they could not and would not free themselves. Eventually, because of it their love suffered also. While the young lady was inclined to see her lover's determination to hold to his views as stubbornness and maliciousness, little by little the young man began to see her as less noble and beautiful than she first appeared to be. It came to a break-up, and it was harsh and painful.

The lady went back to her old world and judged the young man the more harshly since basically she still loved him, and since there were still voices within her telling her that not all the wrong was on his side, and not all the right on hers, and since she experienced hours when she asked herself in deep pain if her place was not at his side after all. But there was no longer a place for her there. In his rejected passion, in his hatred against that which confronted him in his beloved as an obstructive and separating power, he went and entered into a union with another woman. This other woman, who basically had much less in common with him, and who only appeared attractive and good but in reality was just prettified through make-up and experienced in the art of deception, responded with apparent enthusiasm. With zeal she said yes to all his ideals and all his passions—nor did she do so without conviction, for she, too, opposed the existing views and institutions. The youth thus found consolation for the loss of his true love, though only superficially, because the noble figure of the first true sweetheart rose often behind the reality of the much less noble substitute lover. Their relationship led to marriage, and then the tragedy intensified.

Little by little, the nature of the young man's new wife emerged much more clearly: she manifested herself as basically cold, superficial, and sensual, with a stroke of demonism. In his relationship with her, the husband kept losing, almost without notice, his spiritual ardor. And the children born to this union all had a dual character. From their father they inherited an idealism, but from their mother they received base, degenerate, often demonic characteristics. It was as if both a blessing and a curse had been placed upon them. The tragedy reached its climax in a grave family catastrophe in which this false marriage broke up.

Honorable assembly, what I have narrated is, as far as comparisons can be illuminating, the relationship of socialism and a world view that has developed, by and large, on the European continent. We don't want to overlook the fact that it has taken another form in the Anglo-Saxon world and in some ways also in our country; but we are speaking about what has become a decisive reality in our country, about our great tragedy. But the tragedy need not be, and I believe will not be, the last word in this development.

I see socialism as a strong countermovement against the

main tendencies of the era in which it appeared. It is—if I may temporarily use this oft-misunderstood word—basically an *idealistic* movement. With its idealism, socialism, this realm of the soul, this cause of man, this claim of spiritual values, rises above the materialism and mechanism of the whole era, above a world that surrenders spiritual values for material values, people for money, the soul for the machine. When one looks at the whole development, one can honestly say that socialism does constitute an elevation of the soul, of the spirit, of the human being. One could go still further and say that socialism is, without really knowing it, an elevation of God over against a world alienated from him. Indeed, it seems to me that seen from above this is its ultimate meaning.

But now the basic reality that confronts us is the fact that socialism, this intrinsically highly idealistic, spiritually devout challenge to a world of opposing values, has united itself with a world view that contradicts its innermost nature, a world view that is completely destroying it and turning it into the opposite of what it intends to be. That is the tragedy about which I have spoken in the parable. And one's sense of the tragedy increases when one recognizes that it occurred originally much less because of some fault in socialism itself than because of a kind of destiny, a kind of inevitable fortune. Why did socialism enter into such a union in the first place? Because its whole battle to replace the existing world with a new one seemed to call for it.

This will become immediately clear if we now pose the next question: What is the world view with which the part of socialism that is most important for our consideration united itself? That is to say, what views concerning the ultimate basis and purpose of reality did this political, economic, and cultural movement of socialism assume?

I will raise the points that seem most important to me. It seems to me that most important of all is the antagonistic stance that socialism has taken toward religion, and specifically toward official Christianity. For this seems to me to be the basic reality that underlies our whole weighty problem, the tragic fundamental fact of our whole modern Western history. I will be dealing with it only in this aspect, the relationship of socialism to *official* Christianity. It will have to be the task of another to deal with the relationship between socialism and true Christianity.

The tragic reality can be formulated thus: in our Continental cultural circles all progressive movements that were concerned with political, social, and cultural change; with liberty, equality, fraternity, to use with caution this slogan of the French Revolution; with all struggles for justice, for truth, for democracy, for better community—they all had to oppose official Christianity, because official Christianity had, by and large, first turned against them. It was this that created the tragic schism in our history, and from this schism has sprung one misfortune after another. From it there stemmed and continue to stem social conflicts, as well as a world war. But how did this initial rejection itself come to pass?

If I may condense all sorts of developments widely separated in time and space into one symbolic event which, naturally, was of a decisive significance, then I would cite the great Peasant Revolt of 1525, the greatest sociopolitical revolution of the West prior to the French Revolution. At that time Christ and the people were one. The peasants, who demanded their sacred rights as a people, carried on their flags next to that symbol of social progress, the sandal, the picture of the crucified Christ as a symbol of the religious foundation of their movement. They had read in the Bible, which Martin Luther had put into their hands, the gospel of the sonship of God and of the brotherhood of the children of God, and from that they drew with devout enthusiasm the necessary and obvious conclusions for political and social life. They came with these conclusions to Martin Luther, their beloved confidant.

From a human viewpoint, Christ's cause in the West rested in Luther's hands at that time. Only at a few points in history has a man had the scales of world history so decisively in his hand as this man did in that hour. We know what happened. This man, whose greatness and whose work in other areas we do not wish to question, driven in part by an unholy passion, in part by a one-sided distorted truth, broke so thoroughly the bond between Christ and the people that it seems almost impossible to draw them together again. He bound the cause of Christ so closely to the cause of princes and rulers that it now seems almost impossible to break the union. He spoke incredible, thoroughly wicked words against those poor people, curses that echo through history. He shouted loudly that the gospel had nothing to do with worldly things. He declared that revolt was the worst of all sins, and he said worse things yet.

The people and the princes heard Luther's words. The flames of social war flared up. A swollen stream of blood flowed out of the mortal wounds of a hundred thousand peasants, reflecting the thousands upon thousands of villages and towns that were burned, that resounded with the cries of martyred and assaulted children and women. Out of all this leered the face of a new, century-long serfdom. The blood flowed through the Christian West—and since then its stream has separated the cause of Christ from the cause of the people. We, too, confront this stream. If I may say so in a still more general way, the tragedy of our historical development is due to the fact that there are two separate lines that run in it: the line of those who believe in God but not in his Kingdom on earth, and the line of those who believe in the Kingdom of God on earth but not in God.

As far as socialism in particular is concerned, we all know how official Christianity—apart from some noble exceptions here and there—has reacted to it until now. I would like to add just one note to characterize the relationship. Long ago, before the war, a clergyman representative of German Protestantism told the story of the relationship between the church and socialism. He showed how for a long time the proletariat looked again and again to the church as to its advocate, awaiting from her a word supporting its cause, an understanding, an intercession—but in vain. Finally, he summarized this history in two terrible sentences: "What has the proletariat expected from the church? Everything! What has the church given the proletariat? Nothing."

Since this is indeed the case, socialism had to turn against religion, had to call it "the opiate of the people," had to battle it as its deadly enemy, for that is what religion was. Its conscience clouded, religion prevented people from knowing the truth. In particular it prevented the proletariat from knowing the truth. It placed unjust world orders beyond challenge by proclaiming them to be the will of God. Socialism had to fight against this Christianity which became not only a conservative but a downright reactionary power and functioned as a protector of all that was reactionary. It had to fight against this God who desired the status quo, against this Christ of the powerful and mighty. Somehow it had to be so. We would not wish it any other way, for it was not only an inevitable response on the part of socialism, but also a healthy development for Christianity. Christianity needed a radical shake-up. Still, out of all this emerged the tragic union of socialism with actual or apparent atheism and with anti-Christian forces, and out of that developed, as previously noted, everything else.

This becomes apparent right away when we think about the second main characteristic of the socialist world view. After socialism lost in this way its basis in religious faith, it sought a substitute for it and found it in science — or rather in what it understood as science. Science became for socialism the seat of all truth. Science assured the victory of socialism. Marxism, which calls itself "scientific socialism," stated that socialism had to develop out of capitalism by what were alleged to be scientific means, and socialists believed it. It is only a belief, but what a belief! Its whole vigor consists in a glorification of science, and this became a significant mark of the world view of socialism. Marxism strapped to socialism a distinct rationalistic and intellectual bias, a one-sided emphasis on the rational and calculable. The religious ardor, taken from the altar of religion, now burns on the altar of science.

It is a similar story with the third basic characteristic in the world view of socialism, its materialism. When we speak of the materialism of social democracy — and that is now our main concern — we must make a careful distinction between the so-called historical materialism of Marxist theory on the one hand and metaphysical materialism on the other. The former, as we know, is in essence simply a method of interpreting history, the distinctiveness of which lies in the fact that it explains historical developments primarily as reflections of the economic factors of an era. Statements about the ultimate purpose and meaning of the world—or, to put it more precisely, observations about whether the basic element of reality is spirit or matter—are not an inherent part of the philosophy. Metaphysical materialism, however, does take this step: for it, the basic element of reality is matter, and spirit is only a reflection or function thereof. Although one must recognize this difference, I do not consider it to be as decisive as is often asserted. To me the so-called historical materialism (as it has developed, and provided it remains consistent) seems to presuppose a materialistic, or perhaps more pointedly, a *naturalistic* world view. It is a world view that denies the original, creative power of the Spirit, that denies the prior existence of the Spirit. Then there is the undeniable fact that to a large extent metaphysical materialism has become the belief of social democracy. A look in social democratic libraries and newspapers, especially from an earlier period, leaves no doubt of this.

But now I must say this: it is not without reason that materialism arose; in fact, it is almost inevitable that it arose, for it came in reaction to an idealism that was not less false than the form of Christian religion against which socialism fought. When Marx came along, there prevailed in Germany the so-called idealistic philosophy, which was one colossal hymn to the spirit and its lordship. On that form of idealism, represented by Hegel, Marx lighted his fire. This idealistic philosophy proclaimed great things about man and his glory; it made a god out of man. It declared the evolution of freedom to be the meaning of history, and it declared this freedom to be the incarnation of God. But this message did not lead to revolution as might have been expected, despite the fact that some of these thinkers (particularly Fichte, the mentor of Lassalle) made a beginning in this direction; on the contrary, it became reactionary. It didn't attack the world, but clarified it, glorified it. It idealized the existing reality instead of trying to change it through the ideal.

Against this idealism rose up the materialism of Feuerbach and Marx. The views of the latter were basically idealistic, but ideals were to be transformed into reality. The world was to be subdued to the spirit that his philosophy glorified. The philosophers might explain the world, but the world was then to be changed according to the well-known word. The divinity of man was to be realized in matter. That is the original meaning of Marxist materialism and of similar schools of thought. Such materialism is the true child of idealism. In it idealism's great vitality lives on; in it idealism's intoxicating fiery spirit glows. Surely there are valid reasons for its existence.

What has been said bespeaks a truth of another kind. There exists another idealism or spiritualism, a false form of idealizing the world and of representing the right of the spirit, a kind of idealism found particularly within Christianity. Because of its glorification of the inner life, Christianity forgets the spiritless brutality of existing conditions. Because of concern for heaven, it forgets the demands of the earth. Because of service to God, it forgets service to men. This kind of idealism is also found in the optimism and patriotism of the affluent ruling classes, who feel the need to proclaim lofty ideals during sacred or secular leisure hours even though they betray them in the following hours. They idealize the existing world lest someone might want to change it; they like it as it is. When you compare this false spirituality and piety, these idealistic lies with socialist materialism, then again the latter is right. By way of contradicting this false spirituality, it embraces even that metaphysical materialism of a Vogt, Moleschott, and Büchner with all its shallowness and spiritual coarseness. Moreover, when the worker is placed in a situation in which the struggle for bread and for material things becomes the main concern of his life, he obviously has to see his ideals in material goals. For him bread is spirit, one less hour of work is of a piece with the salvation of his soul, and a better place to live represents an important bit of human value. When we realize this, then we can understand the meaning and the necessity of this materialism that is the backbone of socialism.

Taking up another point, we arrive at similar results. If we pursue further what we said about the socialist glorification of science and ask what kind of science it is that is being talked about, the answer will be the natural sciences—specifically, the natural sciences that in the times of the rise of capitalism and socialism were making their well-known victory march. One might say that the world view of socialism became a world view of the natural sciences, though to do so would be to knowingly use a misconception; for a world view is not a science, and science is not a world view. But it is precisely in this misconception that the error of a whole period lies.

Just what is this so-called natural-science world view? One can characterize it briefly by saying that it traces all aspects of reality back to nature. By nature it understands a more or less mechanistic complex of causes and effects. It is causalistic and deterministic. It acknowledges no purpose or meaning to the world; it only describes the cruder and finer workings of the mammoth machine that it conceives the universe to be—a machine in which one may perhaps catch a glimmer of spirit here and there, but which in reality leaves no place for God, for the soul, for freedom, for any genuine spirit, or for any purpose in living.

Again we must say that this world view pushed itself on socialist thinking, the task of which was to devote energy to the mastery of the material world. It sought to explain material things, to investigate their nature, and here the methods of mechanism and determinism recommended themselves only too readily because, for reasons previously stated, the so-called spiritual explanations and methods had already been ruled out.

It must also be added that a mechanistic and deterministic perspective is comprehensible to the modern industrial worker because on the one hand he is bound to a machine that too often is not so much his servant as his master, and on the other hand he is pitted against powers that he stands no chance of prevailing over, powers that rule over him with iron necessity. How in such a situation could he believe in a creative spirit, in freedom of action, in a purpose in the world, in a living God? Obviously these very evident mechanistic and deterministic thought processes had to have an extremely deep impact on the whole world view of socialism.

A mechanistic perspective that is rooted in materialism will tend to put a special value on quantity on the one hand, and on inorganic matter on the other. Materialistic socialism will be characterized by a great love for volume, for big business of all sorts. It will be marked by an imperialistic bent and a scorn for the "little man." It will also lean toward a certain deification of the state and toward centralization, for both of them are products of a type of thinking that does not take into account the real person, the individual, the soul, the personal spirit, the organic life.

Another mark of the so-called natural-science world view of the nineteenth century was its overemphasis on natural instinct as the working power in all of life. Instinct, however, reaches its peak in egoism. Thus, egoism had to become the interpretive principle for the development of the natural and human world. This requirement seemed to be best filled by Darwinism, with its assertion that the struggle for existence is the principle factor in the development of species. If socialism developed a particularly close bond with Darwinism, it did so for different reasons: an opposition to official Christianity, a certain cynical pessimism (which I will soon explain further), and above all, the conviction that Darwinism justifies the theory and practice of the class struggle. The class struggle was contrasted with the above-mentioned false idealism which only glorifies and falsifies reality.

There came a point in time that must be particularly emphasized. It is well-known that along with causalism (which leads to mechanism), the so-called natural-science world view of the nineteenth century included evolutionism, or development theory. We know that Darwinism is only one of its applications and manifestations, and not the most important one. Evolution is definitely closely bound to socialism. In a way, Marxism is a form of evolutionary theory. It is a Hegelian interpretation of history in which thesis and antithesis result in a synthesis through a "dialectical" development, except that it turns the idealistic process into a materialistic one. From this perspective, evolutionary development becomes an almost almighty deity and takes the place of the Christian God.

Even apart from specifically Marxist thinking, however, socialism almost everywhere converges with a continuous and enthusiastic belief in progress. It has turned its face confidently toward the future. It sees everywhere not what is stable and permanent, as does conservative doctrine, but rather what is changeable and transitional. It doesn't look on the calm sea of truth but on a rushing stream, and it puts its trust in the boat carried by this stream to its goal. This progress and victory in the form of development is not brought about by an idea or an identifiable spiritual power that like a guidepost shows the way in and through history; rather, it is brought about by nature.

With this natural-science thinking, both in general terms and in its specific views on evolution, goes another trait of Marxist socialism: relativism. It is dominated by the idea that no human manifestations have a stable, lasting base but that they remain in a continuous state of flux and change. It is in the nature of natural-science thinking to hold that no phenomenon contains anything absolute or self-sufficient, that all reality is reduced to dependence upon opposing restrictions so that each phenomenon is relative to its opposite.

For the natural-science world view, spirit is relative to

matter; it is, in fact, ruled by it. For Marxism, all spiritual values are relative to economic conditions. In incorporating them both, socialism thus loses all absolute significance; it becomes a wave in the flow of history, nothing more. This necessary consequence, though seldom seen clearly enough, stands, of course, in terribly sharp contrast to the Marxist conviction that socialism is the firm goal and therefore the ultimate end of history — just as the natural-science relativism is quite different from the Hegelian dialectic, the innermost tendency of which is precisely to assert a complete truth through thesis, antithesis, and synthesis, and to make the foundation of the truth more and more clear through the relativization of individual phenomena. Again, out of Hegel emerged Darwin. But this naturalistic relativism also expressed an inevitable tendency of the labor movement. It is good to understand that a movement that had to fight against a false antagonistic absolute in the form of the existing social structure and social ideology used relativism as a battering-ram against these walls. "It hasn't always been the way it is now; on the contrary, it has been different, and so it can become different again." Relativism, like evolution, becomes a driving force of the messianic hope.

There is another point through which I would like to express the same idea. Characteristic of the socialistic world view or, as one might better say in this case, of its philosophy of life, is a certain libertinism, a certain contempt for morals that one often (though by no means always!) finds in Marxist socialism. This fact becomes especially apparent in one significant area: the sexual ethic. As is well-known, Marxism takes the accepted views rather lightly. It advocates everything that entails a relaxation of or challenge to traditional strict ways of thinking. It sometimes believes that it must exalt adultery for the greater honor of socialism. If it sets out to work with enthusiasm for birth control and abortion—an enthusiasm that deserves to be spent on a better cause—then, in addition to its libertinism, there can also be seen at work that kind of rationalism and intellectualism that militate against a sense of deeper values and the corresponding ideals of enjoying life and gaining security. The economic bases of neo-Malthusianism, the importance of which I certainly recognize, I shall leave aside. I am speaking now only about that kind of libertinism that celebrates the sort of thing that ought at best to be a terrible necessity. This libertinism, however, manifests itself in other areas of life as well. Many people seem to think that a certain moral looseness—indeed, licentiousness—is a necessary, morale-boosting ingredient of socialist philosophy.

This revolt against morality also has its justifications. For one thing, it reflects the revolutionary character of socialism as a whole. But it is also justified as a repudiation of the lies and corruption that are often connected with bourgeois morality. Libertinism is almost always a reaction against some kind of pharisaism.

Finally, I must complete this picture of the socialist world view (including its life philosophy) with a paradox involving its false pessimism, which corresponds to its equally false optimism.

Socialism is characterized by a certain pessimism, and even cynicism. Since it stands in opposition to the existing orders and must rob them of the appearance of any idealism or divine sanction, it has a tendency to suspect all idealism, to believe in nothing that is good and pure, to degrade and tarnish everything good and pure that does not fit into its mold. That is the means by which one form of socialism battles against the League of Nations and pacifism as well as against all religions and all serious morality. It therefore loves the skeptics and even cynics such as Heinrich Heine and Anatole France, simply because their scorn strikes out at the same society that socialism fights. Thus even Friedrich Nietzsche receives the honor (though he probably would not value it too highly) of being made a saint of socialism. His maxim about "moral-free virtue" is valued by certain Marxist "supermen" in theory and practice as if it were contained in the Communist Manifesto rather than in the writings of the worst scorner of socialism and of all common people. And yet at the drop of a hat this cynical pessimism can paradoxically turn into an equally false optimism that readily sees people as good, explains all human failings simply in terms of social conditions (in this it is similar to Rousseau), and trusts that the natural development of things will make everything all right. This optimism is understandable, too, for socialism is a powerful belief, and where this belief has no deeper foundation, there it must express itself as superficial enthusiasm for progress and development.

Dear assembly, I have tried to present the world view (and the life philosophy) with which socialism on the European continent has for the most part converged. It seemed to me to be right to show a certain inevitability in this union, for only in this way do we penetrate to the tragic depths of the problem. In this assault of socialism on the existing order in religion and morality rather than on just politics and economics, a new world wants to come to light. It is a world that has a great right, a right that goes beyond that which lies just in the consciousness of the bearers of socialism. One must understand this thoroughly if one wants to perceive the promise and the tragedy of this development.

A particularly important insight now presents itself: if one considers the previously sketched union of socialism with that particular world view to be an error, one must not immediately speak about a guilt unless one is speaking about the guilt of a whole period of history. May this insight, which is both burdensome and liberating, fall on the conscience of those more serious representatives of the bourgeois Christian world who are ready to criticize socialism because of the way in which it has been historically realized. The whole period of history in which socialism did not rule, the heritage of which socialism had to accept, must bear the guilt.

Without a doubt, the problem is tragic. That is why from the beginning I have spoken of a tragedy and why I now must return to the theme. I repeat my assertion that the world view (and life philosophy) adopted by the socialism that we see around us does not correspond in essence with that of the real socialism; in fact, I would argue that it contradicts the very nature of real socialism, that it is all a fatal misunderstanding. The picture of that tragic marriage appears again before our eyes.

I will start with the fact that whatever right there was in socialism when it adopted that particular world view turned in time more and more into a wrong. I have alluded at times to this fact, but now I would like to place it in the proper light by touching upon it again. The battle against official Christianity was justified and even necessary—and oh, how much good could have come from it! But how fatal it was when the battle was fought in the manner of a superficial mental enlightenment and barren freethinking when it was presumed that the fight would be advanced by a stupid contempt for the Bible (about the meaning of which the mocker had no notion), by a denial of God and of any higher destiny for man, and even by an attack on the historicity of Jesus, the strongest protector of all socialism, and by a persistent reliance on certain theories that it clings to as expressions of scientific fact even though they have been long since thrown on the junk heap by the scientific community. The assertion of materialism as a new valuation of matter over against a false idealism and spiritualism was justified and necessary, but it was fatal when this originally spirit-filled, so-to-speak religious materialism turned into a spirit-forsaken, spirit-destroying, simplistic belief in matter.

Justified and even necessary were the methods of reasoning that drew upon the natural sciences, which clarify and expound the biological foundations of life, and especially valuable was the emphasis on nature and natural truths over against all conventional lies of bourgeois civilization. But it was fatal when the thought emerged that with such methods the whole meaning of the world and of life could be explained, when the type of thinking surfaced that stifles all creative power of the Spirit, its freedom and worth, calling all human demands based on spiritual worth an illusion and thereby destroying the very roots of socialism. And it was fatal when finally the point was reached at which natural instincts were glorified—instincts that socialism should in fact restrain and purify—and theories were embraced which by their justification of the purely animalistic and disreputable are a mockery of socialism.

Justified and even necessary was a certain theory of development and of progress; fatal, however, was the conversion of this theory into an excuse for inactivity that assumes that history will run itself, that there is no need to shape it through faith and courage.

Justified and even necessary was the relativism that softened a torpid absolutism and replaced a static world with a dynamic one; fatal, however, was the abandonment of all absolute and eternal values without which there is no truth, no world transcendence, no faithfulness.

Justified and even necessary was the optimism that based its faith in man and his future on the belief in a final, victorious truth and power of the good; fatal, however, was the optimism that ignored the demonic powers of human nature and therefore failed to prepare defenses against them.

Justified and even necessary was a certain pessimism concerning a profoundly degenerate civilization; fatal, however, was the degeneration of this pessimism that also served to cut off the roots of socialism and became a diversion for morally corrupt intellectuals who saw the working class as just the right material to be used for their sport.

Justified and even necessary was a repudiation of bourgeois morality with its Mammonism and pharisaism; but it was fatal when it led to a libertinism that competed with bourgeois morality and made of socialism a swamp for those hedonistic amphibians, common mostly among the intellectuals, who believed that they could live out their very unsocialistic drives there without shame.

In sum, the revolutionary impetus inherent in socialism is powerful, and it should be undergirded by an alliance with an appropriate world view, even though it is in this manner—fortunately it is not the only one—that these words are substantiated:

> To the devil with the spirit,
> The apathy remains.

In short, this is what the whole development amounts to: one arrives at exactly the same old world that one wishes to overcome.

Thus we stand, honored assembly, before a paradox: the world view with which socialism has united itself in its battle against the bourgeois-capitalistic world is the very world view held by that bourgeois-capitalistic world. This is what these socialists need to think about a great deal. It is evident in all its aspects. Atheism—is it not a natural doctrine in a world in which God, denied in all sort of ways, is being replaced by Mammon and his image in man is being violated? Materialism — was it not inevitable that it should become the expression of the faith of a period in which the Spirit has been stifled by money? Mechanism —is it not a natural perception of the world in an era in which the machine is everything and the soul, the human personality and its free, creative impulse is nothing? Darwinism (in the sense of a world view of power and selfishness rather than Darwin's scientific hypothesis)—does it not fit a time of imperialism and militarism, of colonial politics and exploitation of the proletariat? Does it not express the spirit of capitalism? Intellectualism—is it not also a fruit of a historical period in which the predominance of technology over people, of calculation over the voice of feeling and conscience, has caused everything truly human to be lost? Skeptical relativism — is it not the fruit of a society that has sacrificed belief in genuine spiritual worth and replaced it with service to sensual idols? In short, is this whole world view not simply the reflection of the world view out of which capitalism, the deadly enemy of socialism, arose, and which, in a reciprocal action, capitalism itself has also recreated? Is this a world view that can befit socialism? Is it not rather its deadly enemy? Is it not in fact no more than the bourgeois world view as it developed after the bourgeois world had gradually lost the religious foundation on which it had formerly rested?

Anyone who knows the ABCs of intellectual history knows that the previously described type of thinking, which converged in broad areas with socialism, originally had absolutely nothing to do with it. It is the thinking of the so-called Enlightenment, especially that of the eighteenth century, and also of the natural-science/technological period—that is, the time in which capitalism arose and reached its peak. One can think of no more tragicomical spectacle than that of socialists insisting that they must express what socialism means to them by ostentatiously professing the bourgeois-capitalistic world view. Should not the same thing that we know only too well in practice, having learned it painfully enough, repeat itself also in theory — namely, that socialism is actually a child of the conditions that it is fighting against, that the weakness, sins, errors, and bad legacy continue to be present in it? Yes, this is the naked, simple truth: the world view of a type of socialism that takes pride in its revolutionary character is nothing other than the worst, most reproachable heritage of the world represented by capitalism. To be truthful, if socialism wants to carry out a revolution, it will first have to carry it out here. If you want to destroy capitalism, you must first destroy this world view on which capitalism is based. Is it not incredible that some of you want to destroy capitalism by strengthening its foundations? No, this revolution, the revolution of the spirit, must come first.

The same holds true for the philosophy of life that belongs to that world view. The unchained instinct—is that not the present world that we as socialists want to replace with another? Is it not the world of egoism, of the drive toward power, of greed—all elements found in capitalism, militarism, imperialism, in war, exploitation, and dictatorship? Is not Malthusianism, the starting point of Darwinism, together with Darwinism itself, the theory that hunger, poverty, and a battle of each against each constitute the driving power behind all development in nature — is the combination not a true mirror of the capitalistic world and actually the precise opposite of socialist thinking? Much more socialistic is the thinking of another great natural scientist who is also a great socialist—Kropotkin. He teaches that the strongest drive in nature and in history has not been the struggle for survival but rather the struggle for mutual support, a teaching that can be documented scientifically far better than Darwin's theory.

Libertinism—is it not the product of a period that has thrown aside all moral norms and forms in order to achieve unbridled self-enjoyment? Is it not simply the laissez-faire principle carried over from the economic world to the ethical world — a false principle of freedom and a right to enjoy life to the fullest? Is that really something new and unheard-of, something revolutionary and socialistic? Moral freethinking, lewdness, degradation of man and woman, fun viewed as the purpose of life, contraception and abortion of the fruit of the body—surely one knew all of this in the bourgeois world well enough and long before socialism came along. When a particular brand of socialism becomes enthusiastic about such things, that is surely nothing revolutionary; it is simply a repetition of the terrible old tragedy in which the failures and sins of the so-called upper classes move downward. And the lower classes, having been thus corrupted, do not respond by mobilizing all their forces for a fight against this penetration of poison among the proletariat; instead, they accept the corruption as if it were a medicine or as a nectar of the gods, and in so doing they demonstrate once again that at heart they are not socialists at all but simply a new edition of the bourgeoisie wrapped in red garb.

Out of the decay of culture caused by capitalism and everything that goes with it, there emerged a pessimistic nihilism; and it, too, is anything but socialist. Likewise that superficial optimism—is it not the credo of free-thinking philistinism? And that rationalism which evaluates human life purely in terms of material blessings and which uses these blessings only to produce some form of heightened pleasures, that rationalism which has lost the ability to stand still in reverence before the basic truths of the natural and moral world—has it not sprung from among the machines, those that also turn people into machines? Does not a kind of obsession with pleasure-seeking arise in a society that fails to quench the thirst for genuine life, inasmuch as it inwardly reduces the value of work and spoils the basic elements of human life in general, thereby closing up the deepest and purest wells of joy? This type of thinking that has no appreciation for the awe-inspiring mysteries that are the foundation of all things—is it not the characteristic quality and the curse of capitalism? Is it not a prime duty of socialism to develop a greater appreciation for everything that supersedes the machine and leads to that which is truly human? Must it not rise above the simple calculations that ultimately demean the worth of a human being—for the worth of a human being is not to be calculated—to an understanding of the holy, which stands above both money and machines? Must it not, in order to find man and brother, also find God and soul? Must it not, in order to find solid ground and a firm footing, root itself in something that is unconditional and eternal? For if socialism stands on the quicksand of relativism rather than on the rock of the absolute, its strength will be weakened and its life threatened. It will then be less in a position to assert itself against "the world" and much more in danger of betraying itself. Moreover, the deepest fountains of enthusiasm and work spring only out of the absolute. Only in the absolute can one believe wholly; only in it can one engage oneself completely.

Again I say: this revolution, the revolution of thought (in the deepest and strongest sense of the word) is absolutely the most important revolution that socialism has to accomplish. It must be the first one in principle even if not in time.

Dear assembly! We are faced by two important facts. As we have noted, because of the conditions in which socialism was realized on the European continent and because of certain inevitabilities associated with its struggle, it was forced to unite itself with a particular world view, which in turn developed from a relative truth into a serious error. That is a fact. However, the other fact is that this world view, when thought through, actually contradicts the essence of socialism as a whole and its individual hopes and claims as well, so that it finally becomes the product and expression of precisely that world which socialism is fighting against. This unusual development, by no means the only one of this sort in intellectual history, had to have consequences, and these consequences could not have been anything but tragic. We have sought to illustrate this double fact through the parable of a mismarriage and the children of this marriage who exhibit the tragic results of the union, possessing both the enthusiasm of the father and the low intellect of the mother. Indeed, this parable seems to portray admirably the whole tragedy of socialism as we know it today.

Socialists will simply never be able to convince the opposition with the methods they have chosen. The type of socialism that we are dealing with here—we are not referring to all its forms —makes the terrible mistake of besmirching what is truly holy in its attempt to battle against what is truly unholy. It battles against a false religion, and in the process attacks the sacredness of belief in God, which is stronger than itself. It fights against a false spirituality and destroys the spirit that alone gives it the right to do so. It condemns a false morality and misjudges the general moral truth upon which it itself rests. The result is that the desecrated holiness turns against socialism. The result is that this holiness, instead of fighting *for* socialism fights *against* it. The result is that socialism loses a large part of the strongest and deepest power of human nature—indeed, it even repels this power, making it into an enemy—a power that would yield an unconquerable strength if socialism would only unite itself with it.

The second effect of this tragic error is that socialism, the leading pioneer of a new world, retrogresses spiritually because of its false ways. The world view that we have outlined is falling apart before our very eyes, and everything that is based on it must fall apart also. Most obvious perhaps is the change in the fate of Darwinism, which even in its original form as a scientific hypothesis fell apart. But even the whole development theory has become a problem. The creative deed, the organic drive, the soul are coming back in their own rights. Mechanism and determinism are restricted to their own domain, the realm of inorganic matter, and thereby freedom is given room. Instinct is being driven from the divine throne. The religious urge stirs with new strength.

The world catastrophe may destroy all simple optimism, but it makes room for the thirst for faith. It is quite clear that this is a total spiritual revolution. The world has had enough — more than enough—of atheism, materialism, mechanism, relativism, libertinism, and the fluctuation between false optimism and false pessimism, even though in its despair it pays tribute to these idols more than ever. People of our time, all those who lead or will lead, are turning to completely different ways of thinking, are turning, if I may say so, away from the gods of the bourgeois-capitalistic-materialistic era back to God. Everyone can see this who does not blindfold himself.

If socialism continues to worship its old idols, it will run into the danger of being burned at the stake together with them. One can already see the change taking place in the brave and truth-seeking young souls of the working class. Socialism must align itself with this change, must renew its life from it—which, in my view, it still can do—or else it will be lost, all of its material interests notwithstanding. "For man lives not by bread alone." But there is a danger that the return to the spiritual realm, to the soul, to God, which actually should lead to socialism, will simply lead back to the old order. Should that happen, the false socialism will have to be blamed. In fascism this danger clearly shows its face, at least to those who have eyes to see.

Another result of this tragic error is the false development of socialist tactics. I would like to emphasize that there is a close connection between the socialist world view and socialist tactics. That is actually self-evident, because the actions of men are determined by the way they understand the meaning of the world and of life. The tactical battles in which socialism is almost destroying itself today clearly stem from a contradiction in its world view. The battle centers in the problem of violence. It is now clear that if one doesn't believe in the Spirit, one must turn to violence, and even more than that, one must glorify and worship it; or, to put it more precisely, to the degree that one does not believe in the Spirit, one must turn to violence and thus give up the democratic spirit....

If I may use again the picture that I used at the beginning to characterize the development of socialism, I would say that the child of the false marriage in whom the tragic mistake is most clearly exemplified is Bolshevism. What was great in it—and what gave it great power to lead people astray—was the mark of a titanic idealism on its forehead and the wild fire in its eye. But in this wild fire Bolshevism revealed its demonic power. It wanted everything or nothing. It reached after the absolute. It wanted, so to speak, to wrestle the Kingdom of God out of heaven, but it tried to do so on the basis of a doctrine of violence. It implicated socialism in historical criminality. It waded in blood. It did all this because it believed in no God and no soul, and yet wanted to have the Kingdom of God and man on earth....

Honored assembly, can this catastrophe be overcome, this tragic development stopped, this menacing dagger sheathed? I believe that it can and will happen, and I believe it sincerely. But how can and will it happen? My answer is that it can come to pass if socialism recovers its true meaning — that is, if it gives up its tie with that world view that doesn't suit its nature, and if it develops a world view that does fit its nature. To say it in another and better way, if socialism wants to live and triumph; it must realize in another way what it wanted to accomplish by joining with that other world view. Let me go on. Socialism must accomplish it by developing its latent idealism, which is its basis and presupposition, and without which it loses its meaning, capitulates, and in the end is defeated by its opponents — as everything is defeated that does not remain true to itself.

Socialism must develop the idealism inherent in its nature. When I say this, I realize that the word *idealism* is taboo in the current fashion of thinking. Nevertheless, I consider it a word that we cannot easily replace, a word that will remain. In referring to socialist idealism I intend something quite specific: I believe that if socialism wants to understand itself, if it does not want to default, then it must consciously ground itself in a belief that affirms the right, the power, and the worth of the spirit. It surely rests on the basic assumption of the sacredness of a human being — of every human being — on the assumption of the absolute worth of the human personality. Without this assumption and this foundation all socialist hopes and claims lose their meaning. But this foundation and presupposition of all socialism has, in turn, a foundation underlying it. That "something" absolute and holy in each human personality that all socialism is duty bound to honor must itself be rooted in a higher realm that is absolute and holy, that is to say, in a world of spiritual values that are absolute. To realize these values is the purpose of each individual life, as well as of mankind as a whole. This basic assumption, too, has its consequences— above all, the consequence of freedom. For without freedom the spirit is not really spirit, and a human being has no moral worth. Therefore, mechanism must never have the last word, no matter how much we need it as a tool. The tool should serve the master; mechanism should serve freedom. Therefore, matter ought not to have the last word either. All materialism has value only if it enhances the worth, the power, and the dominance of the spirit.

In any case, it lies in the nature of socialism that, in contrast to capitalism with its emphasis on the dominance of the machine and of money, it brings honor to the free and creative nature of the spirit, the sacredness of personal life, the deeper powers of the mind, the right of the godly and human....

The new moral world that socialism is striving for—partly consciously and partly in an unconscious turmoil—is supposed to become a reality; but it can become a reality only if it is founded on a spiritual basis different from that which is advocated by the kind of socialism that we are fighting against....

This is, dear assembly, the idealism which, as I have said, is the essence of socialism. This idealism we should bring to light, bring into a sharper focus. Socialism grew out of it; with it alone will it live and triumph. This is the revolution of socialism that we demand. This is the first order of the day....

Thus we come back to the starting point of our discussion. The so-called socialistic unbelief in God and in the spirit was an antithetical stand. Socialism's belief wanted to assert itself in this way against a different kind of belief, a belief that was basically an unbelief. This is a paradox. But this happens often enough, and it makes good sense. It could be viewed as the irony of God who asserts his greatness over against those who try to squeeze his eternal life into their formulas and want to pass as the chief tenets of his truth. Thus, the whole conduct of social democracy was absolutely correct, and in spite of everything we would not wish that in the given circumstances it had acted differently. It had to engage in a monumental work of destruction and derangement; there was a tragedy therein, but this tragedy had a healing purpose.

But now that work has been done. Now that falsehood has been exposed. Now that false Christianity and that false spirituality have been destroyed. Now socialism may — indeed, *must* — show its true face. Now it must display its faith, its idealism. Now it must show signs of the new world that it represents, rather than hiding them behind the mask of the old world. Let us not forget: at one time there lived in the bearers of socialism the heritage of a time that was marked by idealism and faith in the deepest sense. This heritage remained the same in its nature but took on a new form. But now it is used up. Through much reflection, great turmoil, and many upheavals, this spiritual world must now be rediscovered and strengthened; on it alone can socialism rest. Now, through a great catastrophe, both the false form of socialism and the false form of Christianity and idealism are dissolved, and a new combination of their components must—and will—take place. A conclusion has come to a whole span of history, and also to socialism, inasmuch as it belonged to this span. Now a new era is beginning, and with it a new phase of socialism, one that is deeper, stronger, and more likely to succeed.

The tragedy of our situation stems from the fact that socialist idealism did not enter into the marriage with the world view based on natural sciences without doing damage to its soul. We have tried to show the results of this tragic union....

Honored assembly, in the end it is not a secondary matter what kind of world view people or movements have, or what intellectual resources nourish their lives. Driven by a divine spark, which of course is man's dowry, one can storm out into battle and fight for a while, but difficult times may come in which only a correct spiritual compass can show the way. Hours of decision may come in which a person can no longer draw upon a truth that he or she is not conscious of, when only a truth of which one is consciously aware will serve. This hour of decision has now arrived for socialism, a movement that once stormed onto the scene with such youthful enthusiasm.

Honored assembly! If I look with socialistic hope into the future, I see great promise but also great danger ahead. To begin with the danger, it is not impossible that we are moving not into a socialist era but rather into the final victory of capitalism, not into a new freedom but into an unprecedented new slavery. On the one hand, I see a mind-boggling new power of capitalism ahead of me, and I see this power in the service of a new ruling class exhibiting a most brutal will to power and a most arrogant feeling of superiority. On the other hand, I see the masses of people in a slavery, also an unheard-of kind, that will be that much worse if, following the American pattern, the slaves will be properly fed and amused. If this view of the future, this look into hell, does not win me over, it is not because I think that the great masses of people will decide to shake off this yoke because they will clearly recognize their material interests. I could well imagine (and many experiences unfortunately point in this direction) that a clever capitalistic tactic would succeed in satisfying the masses by accommodating them to a certain degree and by keeping a tight rein on them. The Grand Inquisitor in Dostoievsky's tremendously prophetic vision could have been right: he said that the masses would allow themselves to be pacified with bread and miracles (and what miracles!) and would not aspire after freedom if it were the case that there were no Jesus, that Jesus who in Dostoievsky's novel confronts the Grand Inquisitor as the representative of the human souls' eternal, God-given longing for freedom. Or, to put it another way, the masses would content themselves with slavery if there were no spiritual powers that could prevent that terrible development.

But such spiritual powers *are* here. This brings us to the second point that I want to make. Besides the social ferment of our times, and closely associated with it, there is also that spiritual ferment to which I have already alluded. It seeks to restore the world of the spirit, and it does so precisely from genuine spirit. It completely invalidates the world view that socialism once endorsed. There is something like a powerful revolution under way, a spiritual revolution, which will be the last word of the political and social revolution and which will help that revolution to a real breakthrough. In my opinion, it will be in the end a religious revolution. And I think that, on the one hand, this spiritual revolution is moving in the same direction and has the same ultimate meaning as socialism; on the other hand, however, I believe that socialism dare not exist apart from this movement, but must be carried on its rising waves. Socialism must be transformed by this religious movement, and this religious movement must be tranformed by socialism. If I see correctly (and I firmly believe I do), there is a movement emerging inwardly and outwardly and it will not only bring to fulfillment the meaning that was inherent in the original socialism but, through a new union of spirit and matter, it will lead to a new era in history. May I remind you of that decisive historical event that I mentioned at the beginning, and close with this thought: The tragedy of 1525 must be rectified, and it will be rectified.

PART III

The Kingdom
in the Bible
1933–1945

The religious-social movement represented by Ragaz strongly protested against dialectical theology, and was in turn sharply criticized by Barth and other dialectical theologians. In a pamphlet entitled "Reformation nach Vorwärts oder nach Rückwärts?" issued in 1937, Ragaz presented his own attack on dialectical theology.

In the piece, he argues that dialectical theology claims to build on the Bible, the Reformers, and Kierkegaard, but that it misuses them all. He particularly stresses their misuse of Kierkegaard, who, together with Blumhardt, exercised a great influence on his thinking. Kierkegaard opposed the reduction of Christianity to right doctrine; for him Christianity meant an existence, a discipleship. Dialectical theology, however, turned it into an orthodoxy.

In drawing on the Reformation, Ragaz suggests, the dialectical theologians appropriate its weaker rather than its stronger aspects, and overlook entirely its prophetic elements as realized in persons such as Zwingli. They downgrade good works to the point of minimizing the importance of ethics.

Moreover, states Ragaz, unlike Blumhardt, who stressed the living Christ, the new theologians focus on the doctrines of Paul, but they distort his teachings into a pessimism and an overemphasis on individual salvation, thereby creating a gulf between God and man. This might be commendable were it to undercut human idolatries, but a pessimistic view of man does not help man to overcome his idolatries when it characterizes his every effort to participate with God as evidence of pride, titanism, and so on.

Regarding Kierkegaard, Ragaz also makes the point that the Dane was being misused by the dialectical theologians when they tried to base their ecclesiology and their internalizing of Christianity and consequent neglect of social concern upon him (despite the fact that it may appear that he had little social concern himself).

And Ragaz highlights the distinction between the religious-social movement and dialectical theology in their very different interpretations of *the Sermon on the Mount. In this, he stands with St. Francis and various heretical groups who take the passage seriously as something to be lived, to be realized in this world — in contrast to the dialectical theologians who, like Luther, explain the sermon's demands away, use it to show what man cannot do, theologize it, and defer its realization to some future time.*

The following is an excerpt from his pamphlet.

REFORMATION FORWARD OR BACKWARD?

THE GOSPEL IS DIFFERENT. It knows no such slogan as "First faith, then works" or "There is no doing, there is only grace." Everything is more organic, dialectical in a deeper sense. Action has its direct meaning and decisive importance, but the importance of grace is not thereby diminished; its value is debased when the other member, the works, loses its meaning. Not faith *or* works, grace *or* action, but the Kingdom *and* its pursuit. One of the main points of the new reformation must be the restoration of the importance of works.

Kierkegaard was perhaps the first man who, starting out from Lutheran Protestantism (not as a rationalist, but rather as a believer, as a devotee of the New Testament), understood this matter. The truly significant thing is that this insight came from a man to whom faith — above all faith as salvation from destruction by guilt — became the Alpha and Omega of life and action as it did to few others in the history of the truth of Christ....

If we consider further that the return of the dialecticians to the Reformation is, strangely enough, a much-emphasized "return to the church," it becomes clear right away that in this regard they cannot draw upon Kierkegaard, for Kierkegaard's whole battle focuses ever more sharply on a battle against the church. In his brochure "The Moment" he lets loose like a volcano whose passion and force can be compared only with that of the prophets of Israel and the greatest among the prophets since then. But those theologians resolve the problem like this: they explain that this battle, which for Kierkegaard was the center of his mission, was in fact an error; and yet they do not hesitate to use the remainder of his arsenal for their dogmatics, which they then use to restore the church and theology. Regarding this, there is actually little to say other than that people who can do such a thing have nothing to do with Kierkegaard. They themselves could really not do anything else, for if the living God and his Kingdom disappear (even though there still may be some talk about them), then theology and the church step in their place. It has always been that way. But it really should be impossible to take the best from a man in order to build up one's system and then kick him as soon as he himself states what his greatest and most important task is. If someone had so terribly erred about what he himself considers to be the crown of his work and his fight, then his whole theology should naturally be questionable. But we dare assume that it was not Kierkegaard who has erred....

Published in 1942, this pamphlet entitled "Das Glaubensbekenntnis" gives considerable insight into Ragaz's theology. Throughout his life he criticized the perversion of theology into arid dogmas, and yet he never ceased to believe that the faith of the apostles was still true and relevant so long as one could see that the central Christian concept was the Kingdom of God. The following selection gives some of his thoughts on Jesus Christ and on the Holy Spirit.

THE APOSTLES' CREED

QUESTION: What is meant by "crucified"?

ANSWER: The cross is the high point of the incarnation because it leads to the ultimate depth of humiliation. It is not only the central point of history, but also its turning point. On the cross the world is conquered through God, the kingdom of the world through the Kingdom of God, for on the cross God is fully revealed in both his holiness and his love. On the cross God is revealed as distinct from the world. On the cross God is revealed as judge and redeemer. On the cross the demons are conquered and the prince of this world is robbed of his power. In the cross the curse of fate is broken. In the powerlessness of God his omnipotence is revealed. In the cross all the powers of the world and of hell are conquered. Before the cross all idols are overthrown. Before it the swastika as well as the bundle of rods [the symbol of fascism] are shattered. The victory flows out of God's holiness, which is fully revealed in the cross, but it flows even more from his love, which is the fulfillment of his holiness. From the cross comes the highest gift of the forgiveness of sin. On the cross are realized Isaiah's words about vicarious suffering, "Upon him was the chastisement that made us whole, and with his stripes we are healed (Isa. 53)....

...You must look upon the living God, whose greatest act was rolling away the stone from Christ's tomb and thereby from every tomb....

QUESTION: What does "from every tomb" mean?

ANSWER: This is important. One dare not forget that even the resurrection of Christ is not a one-time event that took place in the past, but a continuing event. It is a general resurrection—a resurrection to life of everything that is dead, God's victory over all the powers of the world and of hell. It is an ingredient of our daily faith. Grounded in it, we don't give up anything for lost. Grounded in it, we believe in every victory of right over wrong, of truth over lies, of spirit over violence, of freedom over slavery, of humaneness over inhumaneness. Grounded in it, we believe in the resurrection of everything that has been killed, be it things, humans, individuals, nations. Out of the empty tomb that defeated the cross pours an unending stream of resurrection and life into the world. It is Easter and the Easter faith. Only thus does one understand the meaning of the resurrection of Christ. Thus the open tomb leads into the Kingdom of God. Thus in the living God all death is overcome. Thus Christ is the resurrection and the life. He says, "I live and you also shall live."...

QUESTION: What is meant by the Holy Spirit?

ANSWER: It refers to the power that goes out from the Father and the Son and renews the world. In this sense, he is the Creator Spirit, *Creator Spiritus*. He is the Spirit that leads forward and to the end the Kingdom of God, which became the Kingdom of Christ. He is God as living God, as living Christ. From him springs the marvel. From him come the manifestations reported at Pentecost: flames, truth-speaking, conquest of the spirits. From him come the gifts of grace (charisma) to which Paul and the Acts of the Apostles testify. We should pray for it. We should believe in it. As it is, we believe too little in it. Christianity believes too little in it.

QUESTION: What is meant by the Comforter—the Paraclete—in the Gospel of John, chapters 14–17?

ANSWER: It means, according to Christ's own word, that the historical Christ did not express either in word or in deed all the truth contained in him, that an undreamed-of truth has yet to be revealed by him, that the disciples will do even greater deeds than the Master himself, that in this sense every new truth and power will come forth, that revelation is not finished. There emerge problems in history that did not exist in the time of Jesus, about which he could not speak because people would not have understood him then. In this sense each age needs a new revelation for its problems; in fact, each individual person needs it for himself or herself. And it is given. Revelation is an inexhaustible fountain.

QUESTION: Is that not a daring, even revolutionary, idea?

ANSWER: Yes, it is. The Holy Spirit is the great revolution of the world. Jesus' statement that "You cannot understand it now" certainly means that the disciples were not yet mature enough for some of the ultimate heights, freedoms, and audacities of the truth of the Kingdom.

QUESTION: Can the truth of God spread by itself or can and should man assist in its spreading?

ANSWER: He can and should assist in it.

QUESTION: How can he do this?

ANSWER: Through prayer and action. Through following Christ.

QUESTION: But is it not God alone who brings about the Kingdom? Can man bring it about?

ANSWER: The Kingdom comes from God alone, but man can and should do three things: he can and should wait for it; he can and should pray for it; and he can and should place himself at its disposal. Otherwise, the Kingdom cannot come. It will come only to the extent that these things are done.

Ragaz helped Jewish refugees from Nazi Germany, was well acquainted with Martin Buber and other Jewish leaders, and did some pioneering work in establishing a Jewish-Christian dialogue. The booklet "Israel-Judentum-Christentum" was issued in 1942, and in 1947 it appeared in an English translation published by Victor Gollancz, Ltd. Its central theme is that Judaism and Christianity are two branches of a single tree called Israel, and that they must be reunited by returning to the central truth, to the message of God's kingly rule on earth. The following selection is taken from the final chapter.

ISRAEL, JUDAISM, AND CHRISTIANITY

THE APOSTOLIC COMMUNITY OF CHRIST, originating in the Pentecost event, is still standing on the basis of Israel. It awaits the coming of the Kingdom and in the meantime is living in this expectation....

For a long time this stream of the new world has gone on flowing, although with diminishing force. The concept of the Kingdom remained the purpose and the source of strength of the community until in the third and fourth centuries the stream began to run into silt. Gradually religion appeared on the scene in the place of God's Kingdom. The revolutionary tendency of this Kingdom of God began to stagnate and petrify. Dogma took the place of the message of the Kingdom and of Christ....

Thus Israel was obliterated in Christianity. But not entirely. The glowing force of God's Kingdom and its righteousness not only continue to give all of Christianity a certain warmth, radiance, and power unknown to paganism, but it also reappears again and again in minor revolts or powerful eruptions that reveal the revolutionary character of the Kingdom. Tertullian and the Montanists, the monastics, St. Francis and his followers, the Waldensians and Albigensians, the Wycliffites, the Hussites, the Anabaptists, the Reformers of the sixteenth and seventeenth centuries, the Quakers, Christian communists in all periods, Methodists, Pietists, Christian socialists, both Blumhardts—

these are only a few representatives of the more or less vigorous, more or less genuine eruptions and effects of the stream that flows from Jesus and the Kingdom of God, but also from Moses and the prophets, from Israel through and under the history of Christianity....

Thus Israel diminishes in importance within Christianity. And this is Jewry's permanent claim: it has preserved Israel's last sanctum, *Messianism*, which personifies the faith in the kingdom of righteousness on this earth. That is the mystery of its permanence: it stands as a perpetual exhortation to Christianity and the whole world.

Naturally, it must be pointed out that in Judaism, too, the stream that is Israel has become narrow and sluggish. Here, too, God's Kingdom gives way to religion....

Thus Jewry loses what we should like to call its prophetic significance (not excepting Moses)—which is Israel's essence. As Christianity leaves the way of the New Testament to tend toward dogmatism, so Jewry leaves that of the Old Testament to reach the Talmud. As Christianity moves away from the Kingdom to the church, Judaism moves from the Kingdom to the synagogue, which bars it from its own highest and truest purpose. Thus the sacred kernel stays locked in its hard shell. It remains alive, but it does not grow into the tree whose fruits might gladden the Gentiles. Or perhaps it does bear some fruits, but some of them are bitter....

Through Jewry, too, the stream that is the *Kingdom* keeps flowing from Israel, from the one living, holy God. The greater part of it flows underground, but even then it provides warmth and nourishment. And it does manage to break through occasionally. Again and again, as in Christianity, there arise *Messianic movements,* more or less vigorous, more or less genuine. There is *Hasidism,* a grand, marvelous movement—which, by the way, leads quite close to the Gospels and to primitive Christianity, to the common source of Christianity and Judaism. There is Jewish *humanism,* which among the representatives of Jewry strongly champions human rights in every form (this, in itself, constitutes Messianism). There is *socialism,* strongly supported by Judaism: Marx and Lassalle are descendants of the prophets. From the many names that should be noted, let us mention only two, since they are typical of the development and are generally well-known: Moses Mendelssohn and Martin Buber. And there is also — and this is perhaps the most important thing that has happened along this line —*Zionism.*

But in Jewry, Israel has not quite found itself either. God's Kingdom on earth and its righteousness do not yet constitute the sole and simple creed of the Jewish community. Not even in Zionism. Its sacred fervor has not yet burst out in full force, has not yet penetrated the world. Israel has not been realized as yet.

The fact, as I see it, is therefore twofold. Christianity and Judaism both belong to Israel. Israel lives in both (though only partly), but it is not embodied in either one, let alone in both. It flows through, over, and under both. And it judges both. Israel's presence unites both, makes them allies....

How are the union of Christianity and Judaism to be achieved? The answer cannot be the victory of one over the other, or the conversion (much less coercion) of one by the other; it must come in a different way, by means of a double action: first, by a conversion of each to itself and then by a voluntary conversion to the other. As far as Christianity is concerned, I see this conversion to itself in the recovery of its faith in God's Kingdom, both the Kingdom that has already come and the Kingdom that is to come. This is the point toward which all of Christianity's thinking and working should be oriented. And that means, of course, the recovery of the Messianic way of thinking. And if I, a non-Jew, may be permitted to express my opinion as to the path Judaism would have to travel in order to come back to itself, then I would say that it would have to go back to Moses and the prophets and remove the Talmud from the position of dominance in which it has been placed. Then we could stand right away on a common ground. Martin Buber has notably followed this path, both in his translation of the Old Testament (which he prepared in collaboration with Franz Rosenzweig) and in his magnificent book *Der Kommende,* as well as in all his other works. But he is not the only one walking this path.

This, it seems to me, is the means by which we might solve that tremendous problem we call "Judaism and Christianity." Each of the two separate streams of Israel must first recover its own significance and return to its own character and to its origin —to Israel. Each must thus renew itself from within. In other words, God's Kingdom on earth and its righteousness must once more become the living creed of both Christianity and of Judaism. Then Jesus as Christ will belong to both, for he belongs to Israel— which both will have found again in God's Kingdom. Then the contrast and the conflict between them will vanish; then the divided Israel will be united once and for all. In some ways this has already happened, but it will become universal only in the way here indicated.

*In the 1940s Ragaz issued several pamphlets
under the general title "Die Revolution der
Bibel." In them he interpreted particular sections
of the Bible in such a way as to make them
relevant to the current personal and social struggles of people. In this pamphlet, "Die Zehn Gebote," issued in 1943, he gives a strong social
interpretation of the Decalogue. The following are
selections from his interpretation of the second
and ninth commandments.*

THE TEN COMMANDMENTS

The Second Commandment: The Urge toward Idolatry

QUESTION: What does this mean for us? Surely we don't make
any idols for ourselves today.

ANSWER: ... We are all inclined to build idols and to serve
them. Out of our faith in gold, we build ourselves the golden
calf: Mammonism, capitalism, profit economy. And out of our
drive toward power and violence and our faith in them, we
develop militarism and imperialism. We revere the flag as a sign
of the divinity of the nation. We elevate blood and soil, nation
and race, and even the state to a godly status. Out of our
sensuality rises the idol of prostitution. All of these we elevate to
a cult full of symbols. We serve Baal, who binds people to their
unredeemed nature, to the sex drive, to alcohol, and even to
sport. We serve Moloch, who demands that people be sacrificed.

The fruit of idolatry is always dehumanization of people,
servitude, prostitution, elimination of opposition, decay, and
death. When one remains true to God one has in him all that one
needs: fulfillment, joy, strength, power. God fills with his infinity
the infinite longing of the soul. If man separates himself from
God, however, then his soul is filled with greed, and this greed
seizes everything for itself in order to consume it. On this path a
man encounters others who want the same thing. As long as a
man is united with God, he is bound in freedom. His "I" fits into
God's order and law. As soon as he separates himself from God,
his "I" loses the reins: selfishness awakens and grasps greedily
all around. All this applies to nations as well as to individuals. In

this manner violence and war arise on a large as well as on a small scale. The World War was the fruit of godlessness—not of a lack of religion, but a lack of God.

God, the Lord, the holy God, is peace because he is justice. He wants people. He wants righteousness for each person, and especially for the one who is poor and weak. He holds his protecting hand over him.

QUESTION: What does it mean that God is a "jealous" God and an avenger of sin?

ANSWER: It means something great, something without which the world would have to decay and degenerate. There is a judgment, and God is the judge. The judgment often takes time; the fruit, according to God's own order, must ripen. But the judgment will certainly come. Nothing is more certain. God's holy moral order ("the moral world order") rules in everything and over everything. The deeds of men are not without consequence. Men must give an accounting for them and they must pay for them. The nations must atone for their sins (especially for the lack of social justice) just as families must, and each individual also. This order is more reliable and stronger than the order of nature, which ultimately rests upon it. "Do not be deceived, God is not mocked, for whatever a man sows, that he will also reap." The results of wrongdoing are far-reaching.

God rules as judge over the world. In the world catastrophe he overthrows gods and idols that people have made for themselves. He will bring catastrophe into every life that separates itself from others and goes its own egoistic way without seeking him. Even religion and piety are no protection if they are not based upon God himself and his holy will.

QUESTION: Is it not unjust when children and children's children must suffer for the sins of the fathers, sins for which they do not share responsibility?

ANSWER: It may seem unjust, but it is the highest justice, for it expresses the solidarity of people in sin and guilt. That is the depth of God's order. Its sign is the cross of Christ. The reckoning will not be just with each individual separately; we belong together, and God looks at us together. We are not, therefore, responsible just for ourselves. It is precisely this that makes the seriousness of sin and guilt apparent. But we must not forget the other side of the matter. First of all, judgment is abolished through grace. Grace breaks the curse of fate; it brings liberation and rectification; it brings mercy. Furthermore, blessing and promise depend on faith and obedience that are directed to God.

They are intended for nations just as much as for individuals; they are intended for all mankind. And they work together. There is not only a solidarity of guilt but also of grace. This is the most blessed secret of the way of God.

And finally, grace is infinitely greater than judgment. Judgment reaches "to the third and fourth generation," but grace into the thousandth generation.

The goal of the way of God is his Kingdom and his righteousness, which imply the victory over injustice, violence, poverty, sickness, fate, misery, and death. All who cleave to God, serve him and trust him, share in this promise, remembering that it reaches beyond this world into the coming world, where in the great deliverance every seeming injustice will be corrected, every dark fate clarified, every enigma solved. For God is the eternal God, and he, the just and loving one, the Lord and Father, has the last word.

The Ninth Commandment: You Shall Respect the Truth

QUESTION: What does this mean? Does it refer simply to bearing false witness in a court?

ANSWER: It has a much more comprehensive meaning. It means that the truth is holy. It is one of God's fundamental rules for human community. Without truth the community will fall into chaos and hell, into civil war and international wars. It is only on the basis of unconditional truth, of truth stemming from the divine, that there is a true unity, just as it is only on this basis that there is actual justice; without it there is only coercion and violence. It is only on this basis that there is faithfulness; without it souls decay and communities erode from within. But this truth comes only from God, the one holy God. Besides possessing the holy right to respect, life, and property, each person also possesses the right to truth. Holy is his honor, his worth, his good name, but also his manner, his particular way. If you do not give him this right, you are violating the respect that under God you owe him. If you take something from him, you are a thief. If you slander him, you are a murderer. Guard your tongue and your pen from that. Give him the right of truth and thereby give glory to God....

We should not only avoid witnessing against the truth; we must witness for the truth. And not just in person-to-person relations, but also in public life: in politics, in culture, in religion, in the family, in the nation, in the realm of Christendom, in the family of mankind, in the Kingdom of God. We must engage in the battle for truth. We must struggle for ever more truth. We must oppose all the powers of falsehood. We must be witnesses to truth. That means martyrdom. In particular it means willingness to submit to attack, persecution, misunderstanding and suffering of all kinds, and in some cases even to death itself for the sake of truth. For one must serve truth totally. One cannot be truthful in private life and deceitful in public life. Truth is a whole. We are duty-bound to serve the whole. Truth binds us to God, for truth *is* God.

Therefore, we must not forget: We must not only speak the truth; we must also be true. We must not only proclaim the truth; we must also do the truth.

In "Die Revolution der Bibel" series there is included a pamphlet on the Lord's Prayer, published in 1943. In the introduction Ragaz points out that he believes the central point of the Bible to be the message of the Kingdom of God and its righteousness for the earth. He says he wants people to see the Bible not as a book about the past but about the living and actual present. The following selection is taken from his commentary on the petition "Thy Kingdom come, thy will be done on earth as it is in heaven."

THE LORD'S PRAYER

QUESTION: Is the righteousness of the Kingdom of God only of a political and social sort?

ANSWER: It is *also* of a political and social sort, but it requires divine justice, the justice of the Lord and Father, for all men, and especially for the poor and needy. Basically, it demands that all have equal rights to, and deserve an equal share of, the goods of the earth and the gifts of the Spirit. It calls for a community of peoples in the peace of this justice, a community of people within the nations, a community that will realize God's justice through true freedom, equality, and brotherhood, as Isaiah and Micah express it (see Isa. 2, 9, and 11, and Mic. 4) and as the Sermon on the Mount demands it.

QUESTION: What does the righteousness of God's Kingdom mean over and beyond political and social justice?

ANSWER: It means much more. It means redemption from fate, guilt, sickness, misery, and death. It also means the redemption of nature. It means the redemption of the individual as well as the redemption of the world. But it also means a political and social redemption, and that above all.

QUESTION: Has this redemption already occurred or must it yet take place? Has the Kingdom of God already come or is it yet to come?

ANSWER: Both are true. Redemption has already taken place through Christ, but the final fulfillment of the redemption is yet to come. The Kingdom has come in Christ—he is in the midst of us (Luke 17: 21)—but with the living God and Christ, in the power of the Creative Spirit which is the holy God, it is to come again and be consummated. Therefore we pray "thy Kingdom come."

QUESTION: How is it to come? Through our work or through God's power?

ANSWER: Through both. The Kingdom of God is a promise, and at the same time it is a seed. It is a gift, and at the same time it is a task. It comes from God. People cannot make it; they are to accept it in faith and place themselves obediently in its service.

QUESTION: Is only the individual to do this, or is the community to do so as well?

ANSWER: Both.

QUESTION: Is not the church such a community?

ANSWER: I prefer to say simply "the community."

QUESTION: What is the difference between church and community?

ANSWER: The church is the bearer of religion. The community is the bearer of the Kingdom of God, and this means that it battles for his justice in the world.

QUESTION: And what is the responsibility of the individual in the community (and perhaps also against it)?

ANSWER: One's responsibility is to follow Christ, and that means undertaking his cause....

When you pray, you must not think solely of your private concerns, but must include them in God's concerns. You must pray that on the earth the will of God and not the will of people or demons may be done in things great and small, distant and near; that justice and not violence may prevail; that peace and not war may rule; that man and not Mammon may count; that love and not egoism may prevail; that discipline and cleanliness, not licentiousness and vice may rule; that powers of redemption and healing may flow where there is sickness, misery, and death; that tuberculosis and cancer may be conquered; that unredeemed nature, too, may be called out of demonic drives, battle, and misery into the glory and freedom of the children of God; that the sick neighbor may be able to sleep well; that the God-seeking friend may find him; that the community, the movement, the organization may be blessed; that beams of the comforting and helping light of God may fall into the hell of the concentration camps; and so on, ad infinitum.

Ragaz viewed the parables of Jesus as a description of the Kingdom and the Sermon on the Mount as an expression of its demands. In 1944 he issued a book on the parables, Die Gleichnisse Jesu, from which the following selection on the parable of the wise and foolish maidens (Matt. 25:1–12) is taken. In the introduction to the book he points out that the parables are often misunderstood because they are not seen in connection with the prophets of Israel. Because of this they are given an individualistic meaning, and the social message is lost.

THE WAITING

... The central point of this parable is the warning against false waiting for the Kingdom of God.

QUESTION: How is this to be understood?

ANSWER: First of all, we wish to point out that the parable deals with the importance of waiting for the Kingdom and thus, more generally, waiting for God, although this is not its main theme. There is a basic assumption that it is important to wait for God and his Kingdom. God is not a resting God, a resting truth; he is a living God and an unfolding truth. God not only *is* and *was,* but also *will be:* he not only has come, but is coming and will come. ... One must therefore be awake, eager, careful, prepared. How much has Christianity forgotten this!

QUESTION: Have not Christians in their most serious moments eagerly awaited the last judgment?

ANSWER: Certainly, but that was precisely a false waiting, because then the time spent waiting was not taken into consideration. The interest in the coming of God was fixed on the end, on the day and the hour of his arrival in a broader sense, but it was forgotten that God is always coming and will not come just at the end.

QUESTION: Will there be an end?

ANSWER: Surely. But not only an end. And we will soon see what an important difference that makes. First we want to talk about another form of false waiting, however, one that is more modern. Some believe in the Kingdom of God and think that it is coming but see this coming as an endless line. They believe it is coming in that slow development that people falsely read into the parables of the mustard seed and the yeast. They think that it might not come to an end at all, that it might remain always a goal toward which one strives.

QUESTION: Is that not correct? Does not the Kingdom of God need time? Does not God himself need time? Is that not also what is taught in the parable of the seed that grows by itself? Is therefore patience not necessary?

ANSWER: God certainly needs time. The Kingdom of God certainly needs time. Therefore, one must wait, one must have patience. That is important. But one must also be prepared, and that is still more important. For God is always coming; he will not come just at the end. And, as we said before, God comes suddenly. That is his way: he comes unexpectedly, "as the thief in the night." Therefore, one should be awake, one should watch out. Slow development is only one means by which the Kingdom of God comes. It can also come in a rapid development, in a catastrophe, or in a new creation.

The Kingdom of God is moving toward an end. It is not just part of an endless development that finally dissolves into emptiness, and there is a danger in waiting for it as if it were. There is a danger that one might allow oneself too much time, that one might presuppose a long development when action is called for right now, when God is deciding now and calling people to decide now. There is a danger that one will not watch, will not see God's coming, will not hear his steps. There is the danger that one will fall asleep. This falling asleep can consist in one's accepting the present world because the new world is so distant, in one's going the way of the world while expecting the Kingdom to come later on on its appointed day and at its appointed hour. And then when God comes, unexpectedly, as is his custom, one has no oil in his lamp. One is not prepared. One is surprised and confused. Only then does one try to run to the store to buy oil—that is, one tries to reflect upon things, to think them through. But by the time one does this it may be too late and the doors may be closed. That is the "too late" of the parable....

This form of false waiting can be seen particularly in the watchword of liberalism and humanism. But there is another form of false waiting that plays an even greater and more fateful role. It is the waiting found in pious circles and in the midst of what is called "positive Christianity.".. .

The pious lay groups await the Second Coming of Christ, which they suppose will take place dramatically at the end—that

is, in a broader sense of the word, at a particular time.... Before
this time, they say, there is no Kingdom of God. Before that, the
world has the final word. Before that there must be—*there must
be* —wars, violence, statism, justice in the traditional form, the
order of Mammon, and—who knows?—perhaps also slavery and
prostitution. Peace, God's justice, the overthrow of world powers
and *the* world power can be realized only after the Second
Coming of Christ, when the judgment and the world change have
taken place. To await something like that beforehand is fanaticism; it is against God's counsel and will....

This waiting is one of the fundamental missteps of Christianity and one of the greatest obstructions to the Kingdom of
God. Out of it emerges servility...fatalism...pessimism....

The results of this approach are terrible. Since one does not
believe in the coming of the Kingdom of God until the Second
Coming of Christ, of course it does not come. Since one yields
this world to the devil, the devil gladly takes control of it. Since
one believes only in the evil, the evil naturally wins. In this way
Christianity becomes the strongest ally of evil.

But there is also a subtler form of this false waiting. It
presents itself as a dogmatic theology and calls itself "eschatology." It says, "The Kingdom of God, like God Himself, is so
totally different from the world that it can come only when this
world passes away and the resurrection of the dead occurs. To try
to change the world before that time is fanaticism, utopianism,
titanism, evolutionism, optimism. One needs to accommodate
oneself to the orders of this world, to give to Caesar what Caesar
is due, and to be subservient to the authorities; indeed, one should
not only endure the earthly orders but support and advance them
—for God's sake, for the sake of conscience. All this is based on
Romans 13."

The consequences of this theology are the same as those
resulting from the attitude of the pious. It is only more cunning.
Such a theology is also an ally of evil. It becomes a pillar of
reactionary thought....

QUESTION: Why is this whole form of waiting basically false
and unbiblical?

ANSWER: For different reasons.

First,...we must once again emphasize that the central
teaching of the Bible is not focusing on death and the next world
but on the Kingdom of God and its coming to us. Certainly
thoughts about death and the next world can and should also be
on our minds, but only in relationship to our belief in the Kingdom
and not to the extent that death and judgment develop an

autonomous meaning and become "powers," such that we always stress victory and redemption as the last word at the end of history. As has been suggested before, it is not true that the Kingdom of God does not come until the end. That is not the view of the Bible. It comes also before the end. The whole history is a story of its coming. God is always coming, for he is a living God. He does not rest between the beginning and the end. He is also in the unfolding of events. Christ stands as victor not only at the end; he also strides victoriously through history. He does not come just at the conclusion; the whole of history is also the story of his coming.

Finally, what is most important in this connection is that it would not be possible to understand the decisive coming of the Kingdom — or, what amounts to the same thing, the coming of God and Christ — if one had not understood it beforehand and if one had not had the opportunity to experience their coming. Only in correct waiting does one come to understand the correct fulfillment. The correct waiting is, however, no idle waiting; it is an active waiting. Only if we comprehend the task that God gives us today can we understand what God's will is, how he will accomplish his work, how he will come....

...The foolish maidens slept. They are the picture of a Christendom and Christianity that does not wait correctly for the Lord. They simply wait and do not really work, or they do the wrong work. That is the central meaning of the parable of the maidens.

Near the end of his life Ragaz wrote a seven-volume series of books interpreting the Bible and relating it to contemporary events. The series, entitled Die Bibel — eine Deutung, *was written primarily for lay people. In the introduction Ragaz states that he does not claim to be a biblical scholar but is simply searching for the biblical message for his life and sharing his life experiences and struggles with his readers. The series was published posthumously. The following selections are two excerpts from Volume IV,* Die Propheten *(1948), and one excerpt from Volume V,* Jesus *(1949).*

THE BIBLE: AN INTERPRETATION

Prophets and Politics

POLITICS STANDS AT THE CENTER of prophetic activity. This is a reality that the congregation, in whose sanctuary the Bible rests the whole year on the pulpit, definitely needs to realize.

What does it mean to the prophets to take this stance toward politics?... It means, first of all, something general and very important. For the prophets, as in the whole Bible, the relationship to God is not a private matter but rather a communal matter; in the Old Testament in particular it is a matter of the whole people.

Another point accompanies this one. In the relationship to God there is no area that is excluded; his will and command apply everywhere. Whoever departs from this line falls immediately into the realm of Baal.

As a result, the prophet feels deeply responsible for his people. Therefore it is appropriate to consider what kind of people this is. It is, of course, Israel, the people of God, the people that have a special mission, the people that belong to the one holy and living God and are totally bound to him. The cause of God upon earth depends in a decisive sense upon the behavior and the fate of these people. The responsibility before God, therefore, clearly becomes responsibility for the people.

Before the people the prophets represent God, his counsel and his will. They keep watch to see that his will is being done by and through the people. This watch-keeping is the sign the prophets choose again for their commission (see Ezek. 33:1–9)....

Thus, theocracy comes again into the picture. But it is no longer the priest or the king but the one who was freely chosen by God who represents him. Consequently, a time returns when the immediate presence of God is realized, a presence characterized by the rule of a Judge, and thereby a presence characterized by free leadership. God is to be the true leader. It is a free, lay theocracy that appears with the prophet....

In contrast to the Greeks and Romans, the prophets adhere to a holy anarchism. This has been a characteristic of the prophet always and everywhere. No glorifier of the state has ever been a prophet. God alone is Lord —*soli Deo gloria*. It is not by chance that opposition to the totalitarian states represented by Louis XIV and Karl II was expressed in a revolutionary way by Calvinism, which affirms this *soli Deo gloria* in a special way and which is more filled with the spirit of the Old Testament, and especially with that of the prophets, than any other group. (The state always leans toward totalitarianism.)...

From this basic outlook of the prophets there follows a perspective of the greatest importance: democracy. The prophet is a man of the people in the narrower sense of the word: he is the defender of the people, God's representative. There is a mysterious connection between God and the people. The intercession for the rights of the people is thus a significant characteristic of the prophet — always and everywhere. That a prophet might be an aristocrat, in the political and social sense of the word, is unthinkable. When one separates himself from the people, one is no longer a prophet.

This also accounts for the stance of the prophet relative to those in power—to the king, to the officials, to similar persons in power. We are aware of the absolute disregard of the prophets for those who possess such worldly powers and, as a matter of fact, for all who possess power. There is no hint of devotion to them. Without any presumption, the prophet is immediately filled with a sense of superiority over the great ones. To him, there are no great ones. God alone is great. Whoever makes himself great in a worldly sense is small in the eyes of the prophet. The prophet is filled with the greatest respect for people as such, and especially for the weak and despised, but is completely without reverence for the king and the court. The king and his officials are employees of God and of the people, nothing more, and they are accountable to them — even to simple farmers like Elijah and Amos, and to simple city dwellers like Micah (see 1 Kings 21). And the king knows it, too. He makes himself subservient to the prophet, no matter how much it goes against his will. Or he kills him....

This superiority of the prophet to the worldly powers is a characteristic mark and an inevitable criterion. Whoever submits in some way to those in power, whoever shies away from representing the people over against them, may be this or that, but he is no prophet. When Luther confronted the peasants as he did, in league with the nobles, he threw away the role of the prophet along with theocracy and democracy. He planted in his people and in his Christianity the seed of despotism on the one hand and the seed of servitude on the other, and these grew into a tree the fruits of which are poisoning the world....

Human rights go back to the prophets. No preacher or philosopher created them or discovered them. The prophet is the perpetual protector of the rights of God and the people. This is his commission. When these rights are violated, a flame flares up in him that comes from the holy Lord and God. This is true everywhere and at all times — in Carlisle as in Amos, in Henry George as in Moses. Time and again the violation of human rights is at the center of the prophet's reprimand in the pronouncement of judgment....

It is quite understandable that when justice is so greatly emphasized, the opposite of justice, namely violence—and above all the violence against the small and the weak — is most vehemently condemned, both in relations among nations and within them. The appearance of Elijah before Ahab and Jezebel to address their act of violence against Naboth is the most striking example....

Politics in the usual sense is above all worldly-oriented. In one way or another it has to do with the state. It depends on appropriate means, mostly force. No politics, not even of the noblest kind, completely obliterates this rule. But since the prophet confronts this reality, his political activity denotes the abrogation of politics. Where God rules, the state ceases to exist.

From this follows the fact that the prophet always and without exception comes into conflict with the state and its representatives, even where statehood is barely organized or where it exists more as an elementary principle, as "power," as it did in Israel. Thus, Elijah stands against Ahab, Isaiah against Ahaz, Jeremiah against Zedekiah, John the Baptist against Herod, Knox against Mary Stuart, Tolstoi against the Czars. The prophet represents God and his lordship over against the state and its lordship.

However, the prophet represents the justice of God not only over against the powerful, but also over against the people. He is, as we have shown, a God-appointed advocate of the people, a people's tribunal ordained and commissioned by God, but he is no demagogue. In general, the simple people are more receptive to the work of the prophet than to the work of those possessing power and authority, but they are unstable. If the prophet thinks and acts differently than they think he should, then their "Hosanna" changes remarkably quickly into "Crucify him." It is a characteristic of the true prophet that he can go in God's name against the people, against their errors, their passion, their religion, their patriotism, whenever it is necessary. Thereby he renders a great service to them, a service that he alone can render. The prophet is the strongest opponent of tyrants, but also of demagogues....

We can see how difficult this position of the prophet is, and how impossible without God. To the politicians and the army men, the prophet who refers to God and the will of God appears to be a fanatic and a dreamer, and yes, even a madman—and this despite the fact that on festive occasions they, too, confess their faith in God. Or to put it in the context of our times, the politicians and the army men may acknowledge and honor the Bible, too, but any seriousness about biblical ideas only serves to arouse their scorn. They are "realists" and "realistic politicians."

But now we stand before the paradoxical fact that we can speak of the realism of the prophets—that is, about the fact that these fanatics, dreamers, and madmen perceive the reality much better than the "realists" do....

How is this better understanding to be explained? Are the prophets simply more gifted, superior politicians who pay greater attention to the facts and are better informed?

The key lies elsewhere. It lies in the one place that it can lie: in the fact that the prophets see more clearly because they possess the perspective and the sense of truth. These they have from God. Therefore, they stand above the fog in which the others grope and fall into the abyss. They are sobered by God, and thus they do not succumb as the others do to the frenzy of the world, of patriotism and militarism, of ambition, of the greed for power, of pride and hate....

The prophet is, if we may this once use a debased expression, nationally oriented. He is deeply rooted in his people, deeper than the whole patriotic front — the politicians, the military, the priests, the pseudo-prophets, or even the people — because, stimulated by God (the true God, not the national and patriotic God), he carries his people in his heart. He feels responsible before God for them. Because of the penetrating perception that he has received from God, he understands the mission and the task of his people, the meaning of their existence, their right to existence, God's way with them. But with this same perception he recognizes also the mistakes, the dangers, the sins that they fell into—and he perceives both incomparably better than the others.

The prophet is neither a nationalist nor a patriot, because his relationship with the people is determined by God, the one holy and living God. In the final analysis, it is God who counts, not the people. God is not here to serve the people, as every Baal religion (including the Jewish and Christian varieties) claims; rather, the people are here to serve God. Therefore, the people's significance and their right to live—yes, even their lives—depend on whether or not they follow God's way. Therefore, God rejects even his chosen people if, under the appearance of a zealous service to God, they actually serve Baal. Therefore, the prophet opposes the nationalistic pride, nationalistic self-righteousness, patriotic deceit, and patriotic frenzy of his people and their leaders by proclaiming the truth of God. He is their judge and thus their savior. Through promise and hope he raises them from fear, need, despair, and catastrophe, and through his own defeat creates the conditions for the resurrection, becomes himself the assurance of it. So it was in Israel, so it has always been, and so it will always be. There is no purely nationalistic prophet....

Because of the one living God, the prophet becomes interested in other peoples....He knows and feels with elementary power that they, too, belong to God....He stands for individual human rights as well as for the rights of nations....

The Prophets and the Social Problem

It is a well-known fact that the prophets of Israel were preachers of social repentance. This role of theirs is better known than their role as political leaders in the narrower sense....

We are faced with this fundamental fact concerning the prophetic attitude as well as the biblical way of thinking in general and the historical development emerging from that way of thinking, and yet it is one of the greatest paradoxes of the Bible. The poor, oppressed, deprived person—we can also say the weak and lowly person—stands in a special relationship to God. To God, such a person is especially holy. He stands under God's special protection. He has his special promise. The sin against him is a special sin that calls forth God's anger and judgment in a special way, thereby calling forth also the anger and words of judgment from him who stands nigh to God and represents his law—that is, from the prophet....

The goods of the earth belong to God, are holy to God. Therefore, they belong to all. There is no absolute human right to property in God's eyes; all property is rental property. It follows from this that all accumulation of property in one hand (to say nothing of monopolies), every privilege of this sort, is a sin against God. Out of this conviction stems the prophets' indignation against the crass distinctions between rich and poor, their one-sided opposition to the rich, their "woes" against them — attitudes that culminate in Jesus' warning "Woe to the rich" (Luke 6:24) and in his parables about the rich grain-farmer and about the rich man and poor Lazarus....

With this attitude toward the poor, an element of great significance entered into history, an element of world revolution. We can call it "Ebionism." Ebionites (i.e., the poor) are the representatives of this class of people in the Old Testament. They, and not the great and the mighty, are the ones upon whom God's protection and blessing rest. They are the bearers of his cause, not the priests, scribes, and pseudo-prophets. They are the ones most receptive to his command and promise.

We can also say it in a more general way: the people — the simple, working, suffering people—become in this way the domain of God and the bearers of his cause. The democracy of the prophets is thus fulfilled; here, in this holy place, God and the people come together. In Jesus this development reaches its ultimate height and depth.

This line of Ebionism, the poor and lowly, "the people" (in this sense), penetrates the New Testament, and from there it enters with great power into history, emerging in ever new secular social revolutions that point to God.

But the prophets are moved not only by the neglect and oppression of the poor, but also by all kinds of debasement of life in the area that we now call the social ethic. Such debasement must of necessity crop up where the foundations of life have been turned into disorder and have deviated from God's order....

At the close of this sketch of the social message and the social battle of the prophets (and it is no more than a sketch), this question forces itself upon the mind: How does this message relate to socialism and vice versa? Do we or do we not find socialism (and perhaps communism) in the perspective of the prophets?

The answer must be the same as that given in our discussion of the law of Moses, which, we emphasize again, is in its breadth an expression of the prophetic spirit. The answer must be both No and Yes. It must be No if by socialism (or communism) we mean a particular complete program of a party. It must be Yes, however, if we are referring to the meaning and spirit of socialism (or communism) with all its foundations and ultimate implications. This is the socialism (and communism) of the Bible, the socialism (and communism) of God.

From this source (the New Testament continuation included) there emerges what has appeared in the world as effective socialism (and communism). Out of pagan thought, as we have pointed out, social rebellions arose, and from it systems emerged that one could definitely call socialistic or communistic — as recollections of the lost paradise — but no lasting social or socialistic revolution came out of it. This is because the attempts have lacked the belief in the one holy and living God and his Kingdom of righteousness for the earth with the sacred right of people, especially of the weak and lowly, the belief in the role of the poor as the bearers of God's cause, the belief in the deep bond between God and the people. Both Ebionism and Messianism are lacking.

Marxism, too, arose out of Ebionism and Messianism. On that point there can be no doubt among the unbiased. It is no accident that Karl Marx is a great-grandson of the prophets of Israel. Marxism is secularized Messianism. That is its *great* meaning. Only if one understands that does one understand Marxism.

There are still two things to be said. First, the Messianism of the prophets is still incomparably higher, incomparably broader, incomparably deeper than any Marxism: it is as high, wide, and deep as God himself. Second, socialism must return to this, its source, if it is to live, become vibrant, and become victorious.

The Kingdom of God and the Works of Men

1. What do the works of men have to do with the Kingdom of God and in the Kingdom of God?

This is the basic problem in the cause of Christ that runs throughout all of history. Twice it reached representative high points in the battles between Augustine and Pelagius and Luther and Erasmus, but it has also appeared in a thousand other forms, most recently in the battle between dialectical theology and the religious-socialist movement. This battle came to a head in the conflict about freedom of the will, which one side denies and the other affirms — perspectives that led to pessimism in the valuation of man and his history on the one side and to something that one can at first call optimism on the other side.

There are two things that should be noted: the one side relies primarily on Paul, and the other side relies primarily on Jesus and the prophets. The one tends to emphasize the church and religion, and the other is almost always associated with the proclamation of the Kingdom of God.

Where does Jesus stand with his message? Since it is the message of the Kingdom of God, one might at first assume that it is on the second side, but in doing so one would be overlooking a characteristic feature of the gospel—namely, that it transcends the conflicts that have torn theology and dogma asunder, that it rises beyond them and over them and proclaims the wholeness of God. It is the antinomy and the polarity of the gospel that gives it its liveliness.

The Kingdom of God as it is described in the gospel is primarily the affair of God. It comes from God. It is the lordship of God whose will alone should rule, should be done on earth as in heaven. The Kingdom must *come;* it cannot be *made*. It is a gift, not something one earns. But this basic view is juxtaposed with a diametrically opposed position. Besides being an affair of God, the Kingdom of God is also presented as being an affair of men. The gift is also a responsibility; what is given is also something that is earned. One can express it in terms that sharp. Even the coming of the Kingdom is a human affair. It is being prepared, it is being offered, but it will not come if there are no people who are waiting for it, praying for it, working for it, fighting and suffering for its coming. And so the Kingdom comes not just in receiving but also in giving....

It is quite clear that the gospel places a very high value on human action. This is, as we have shown, decisive for the coming of the Kingdom. Two-thirds or three-fourths of the gospel, if one may express it this quantitatively, speak about the action of people....

If action is decisive according to the gospel, then the failure to take action is even more decisive. It is a basic element of the Bible that God places man in a position where he has to decide. He has the choice between good and evil, between obedience and disobedience, between God and the world. This is true of the individual as well as of the nation. Upon this decision one's fate depends. Upon this decision depends the cause of God in the world....

2. Now that this has been clarified, the question arises about the form of Jesus' moral message. Did Jesus teach a new ethic? Can the moral truth that he taught be called just a "morality"?

That would be a misunderstanding of its nature. Jesus teaches no ethic and no "morality"—neither an old one nor a new one. *Ethics* suggests a philosophical system; *morality* suggests a closed, more or less systematic concept, but in any case a concept expressed in a legal form....

Jesus teaches a new *type* of righteousness, not a new righteousness or even less a new ethic. He teaches a new way of doing good stemming out of a new way of understanding God, a new revelation of God as the Lord and Father. Not only is this new form not a system, but it is not a law either, in the sense common to the laws of "those of old." Rather it is the will of God — an always active, always direct will, a will stemming from his holiness and his love. It is the royal freedom of the children of God....

The "ethic" of Jesus is, in one word, the "ethic" of the Kingdom of God; or it might be better said the other way around: the Kingdom of God *is* its ethic. It is the responsibility of the disciple. It is his action. Or let us say it still more correctly: a disciple's action is not revealed in an ethic, but rather in following Christ.

Selected Bibliography

Books by Ragaz

Die Bergpredigt Jesu. Bern, 1945.
Die Bibel —eine Deutung. 7 vols. Zürich, 1947–50.
Dein Reich komme [sermons]. 2 vols. Basel, 1908.
Die Geschichte der Sache Christi. Bern, 1945.
Die Gleichnisse Jesu. Bern, 1944.
Der Kampf um das Reich Gottes in Blumhardt, Vater und Sohn —und weiter! Erlenbach, 1925.
Leonhard Ragaz in seinen Briefen. 2 vols. Hrg. Ch. Ragaz, M. Mattmüller, A. Rich. Zürich, 1966–83.
Mein Weg. Eine Autobiographie. 2 vols. Zürich, 1952.
Das Reich und die Nachfolge. Bern, 1938.
Von Christus zu Marx—von Marx zu Christus. Wernigerode/Harz, 1929.
Weltreich, Religion und Gottesherrschaft. 2 vols. Erlenbach, 1922.
Die neue Schweiz. Olten, 1917.

Pamphlets by Ragaz

"Das Evangelium und der soziale Kampf der Gegenwart." Basel, 1907.
"Das Glaubensbekenntnis." Zürich, 1922.
"Israel-Judentum-Christentum." Zürich, 1943.
"Reformation nach Vorwärts oder nach Rückwärts?" Zürich, 1937.
"Sozialismus und Gewalt." Olten, 1919.
"Das Unservater." Zürich, 1942.
"Die zehn Gebote." Zürich, 1943.

Books about Ragaz

Herkenrath, Silvia. *Politik und Gottesreich. Kommentare zur Weltpolitik der Jahre 1918–1945.* Zürich, 1977.
Jägar, Hans Ulrich. *Ethik und Eschatologie bei Leonhard Ragaz.* Zürich, 1971.
Lejeune, Robert. *Leonhard Ragaz. Bibliographie seiner Werke und Schriften.* Bern, 1951.
Lindt, Andreas. *Leonhard Ragaz. Eine Studie zur Geschichte und Theologie des religiösen Sozialismus.* Zollikon, 1957.
Martin, Johann Stähli. *Reich Gottes und Revolution. Die Theologie des religiösen Sozialismus bei Leonhard Ragaz und die Theologie der Revolution in Lateinamerika.* Hamburg-Bergstedt, 1976.
Mattmüller, Markus. *Leonhard Ragaz und der religiöse Sozialismus. Eine Biographie.* 2 vols. Zürich, 1957–68.
Steinem, Ulrich von den. *Agitation für das Reich Gottes. Zur religiös-sozialen Predigtpraxis und homiletischen Theorie bei Leonhard Ragaz.* Munich, 1977.
Top, M. J. *Religieus socialisme contra national socialisme.* Kampen, 1977.